lonely planet

SINGAPORE

CONDENSED

 Rachael Antony

LONELY PLANET PUBLICATIONS
Melbourne • Oakland • London • Paris

contents

Singapore Condensed
1st edition – October 2002

Published by
Lonely Planet Publications Pty Ltd
ABN 36 005 607 983
90 Maribyrnong St, Footscray, Vic 3011, Australia
www.lonelyplanet.com or AOL keyword: lp

Lonely Planet offices
Australia Locked Bag 1, Footscray, Vic 3011
☎ 03 8379 8000 fax 03 8379 8111
e talk2us@lonelyplanet.com.au
USA   150 Linden St, Oakland, CA 94607
☎ 510 893 8555 Toll Free 800 275 8555
fax 510 893 8572
e info@lonelyplanet.com
UK   10a Spring Place, London NW5 3BH
☎ 020 7428 4800 fax 020 7428 4828
e go@lonelyplanet.co.uk
France   1 rue du Dahomey, 75011 Paris
☎ 01 55 25 33 00 fax 01 55 25 33 01
e bip@lonelyplanet.fr
www.lonelyplanet.fr

Design John Shippick Maps Jack Gavran & Chris Thomas
Editing Bridget Blair & Marg Toohey Proofing Marg
Toohey Cover Jenny Jones Publishing Managers
Diana Saad & Katrina Browning Thanks to Charles
Rawlings-Way, Chris Love, Gabrielle Green, Indra Kilfoyle,
James Hardy, Jane Thompson, LPI, Nicholas Stebbing,
Rowan McKinnon, Victoria Harrison, Shelley Muir

Photographs
Photography by Glenn Beanland. Other photos by
Manfred Gottschalk (p.10), Richard I'Anson (pp. 46,
51 & 59), Oliver Strewe (p. 48), Steve Simonsen (p. 58)
and Veronica Garbutt (p. 59).
All of the photographs in this guide are available for
licensing from Lonely Planet Images:
e www.lonelyplanetimages.com

Front cover photographs
Top Looking up to the tall buildings in the city.
(Richard I'Anson)
Bottom Singapore's future premier Arts facility:
Esplanade – Theatres on the Bay. (Glenn Beanland)

ISBN 1 74059 385 5

Text & maps © Lonely Planet Publications Pty Ltd 2002
Grateful acknowledgement is made to Penguin Books
Ltd and Faith Evans Associates for reproduction permis-
sion: Excerpt from Mammon Inc (pp25-6) by Hwee
Hwee Tan (Michael Joseph, 2001), copyright © Hwee
Hwee Tan, 2001
Photos © photographers as indicated 2002
Printed by The Bookmaker International Ltd
Printed in China

All rights reserved. No part of this publication may be
reproduced, stored in a retrieval system or transmitted in
any form by any means, electronic, mechanical,
photocopying, recording or otherwise, except brief
extracts for the purpose of review, without the written
permission of the publisher. Lonely Planet, the Lonely
Planet logo, Lonely Planet Images, CitySync and eKno are
trade marks of Lonely Planet Publications Pty Ltd. Other
trade marks are the property of their respective owners.

Although the authors and Lonely Planet try to make the
information as accurate as possible, we accept no
responsibility for any loss, injury or inconvenience
sustained by anyone using this book.

how to use this book

SYMBOLS

⊠	address
☎	telephone number
Ⓜ	nearest MRT station
🚌	nearest bus route
🚢	ferry
🚡	cable car
⊘	opening hours
ⓘ	tourist information
Ⓢ	cost, entry charge
e	email/website address
♿	wheelchair access
⚲	child-friendly
✕	on-site or nearby eatery
V	good vegetarian selection

COLOUR-CODING

Each chapter has a different colour code which is reflected on the maps for quick reference (eg all Highlights are bright yellow on the maps).

MAPS

The fold-out maps inside the front and back covers are numbered from 1 to 6. All sights and venues in the text have map references which indicate where to find them on the maps; eg (3, M4) means Map 3, grid reference M4. Although each item is not pin-pointed on the maps, the street address is always indicated.

PRICES

Price gradings (eg $10/5) usually indicate adult/concession entry charges to a venue. Concession prices can include senior, student, member or coupon discounts.

AUTHOR AUTHOR !

Rachael Antony

As the daughter of a pseudo secret agent Rachael had to learn how to live on the run... er, move, from a tender age. This early training (in safe breaking, self defence and the art of disguise) was to prove invaluable to her later in life as a travel journalist. Now based in Melbourne she works as a freelance writer for various lifestyle magazines.

Many thanks to Sam Cordell for taking care of me; and Dennis She, Tricia Lee, Jean Lai and Kelvin Seah for helping out with odd requests. Kisses to the dedicated and talented Condensed team for all their efforts, authors Alex, Dani and Niki for handy hints, Lushi for his fabulous pre-departure briefing, and Laurence – for everything.

READER FEEDBACK

Things change – prices go up, schedules change, good places go bad and bad places improve or go bankrupt. So, if you find things better or worse, recently opened or long since closed, please tell us and help make the next edition even more accurate. Send all correspondence to the Lonely Planet office closest to you (listed on p. 2) or visit e www.lonelyplanet.com/feedback.

Lonely Planet books provide independent advice. Lonely Planet does not accept advertising in guidebooks, nor payment in exchange for listing or endorsing any place or business. Lonely Planet writers do not accept discounts or payments in exchange for positive coverage of any sort.

facts about singapore

Singapore sometimes feels like a city that has tried to bury its own past. Sticky historical truths or quaint but decrepit buildings have no place in modern Singapore, which pursues economic success, social cohesion and prosperity at all costs. At first glance it appears shockingly modern and surreally anonymous, but Singapore is an undeniably Asian city with Chinese, Malay and Indian traditions from feng shui to ancestor worship creating part of the everyday landscape.

However, no amount of bulldozing, development or sanitisation can squelch the uniqueness of Singapore. Singapore-ness is a hardy, rubbery, slippery thing that appears where you least expect it and thrives on contrast. You might spy an old man in pyjamas dozing a mere stone's throw from the uber-swish Raffles hotel or you might stumble across a teenage girl tottering on three-storey platform shoes earnestly tossing fortune sticks at a Buddhist temple. One day you're

in a hawker stall melting in an inferno-like steam cloud over a $2 bowl of Indian curry, the next you're enjoying high tea in whispered environs complete with air-con, starched linen table cloths and gliding waiters.

Singapore boasts some of the world's best shopping, its cuisine is sublime, the people are friendly, it's mega-clean and super-safe, and when you've had enough of the city you can always escape to a park for a quiet moment. Singapore is also truly multicultural – where else can you explore slices of India, China, Malaysia and the Arabic world within a 10km radius? Forget everything you've ever heard about Singapore and explore it for yourself.

Oh what a night! Looking over Boat Quay and the Central Business District.

HISTORY

Malay legend has it that long ago a Sumatran prince visiting the island of Temasek spotted a lion while sheltering from a storm. The good omen prompted the prince to found a city there called Singapura (Lion City). Actual records of Singapore's early history are patchy – originally it was a tiny sea town squeezed between powerful neighbours Sumatra and Melaka. Officially Singapore's history begins in 1819 with the arrival of Sir Stamford Raffles, who was declared Singapore's founder in the 1970s in order to 'neutrally' settle rival claims by local Malays and Chinese.

Stamford Raffles

Raffles, cultural scholar, Singaporean colonist and founder of the London Zoo, died at the age of 45 from a probable brain tumour after suffering from extended bouts of fierce and incapacitating headaches. Having fallen out with the East India Company, his death was ignored by London society. However, many years later on the other side of the globe Singapore marked the 175th anniversary of Raffles' landing with much celebration.

Colonial Conquest

In the late 18th century the British began looking for a harbour in the Strait of Melaka which would usurp their Portuguese and Dutch competitors and secure them lines of trade between China, the Malay world and India.

The young Sir Stamford Raffles arrived in Singapore 1819 and found the empire of Johor divided with two contenders for the sultanship. The Dutch favoured one candidate so Raffles threw his support behind his rival, Hussein, proclaimed him sultan and clinched the deal by signing a treaty with an eminent *temenggong* (senior judge). Thus Raffles obtained the use of Singapore in exchange for modest annual allowances to Sultan Hussein and the temenggong. This exchange ended with a cash buyout of the pair in 1824 and the transfer of Singapore's ownership to Britain's East India Company.

Raffles' first and second visits to Singapore in 1819 were brief and he left instructions (including plans to

Stony-faced Sir Stamford Raffles.

divide the city into ethnic neighbourhoods) and operational authority with Colonel William Farquhar, formerly Britain's chief representative in Melaka. Three years later, Raffles returned to the once-thriving colony and found it in chaos. He sacked Farquhar and replaced him with John Crawfurd.

Early Days

Singapore was soon teeming with Chinese immigrants and the Brits forged good trading relations with the Straits-born Chinese-Malay, or Peranakan, who found an identity in the Union Jack, British law and citizenship. The early years were difficult, marked by bad sanitation, disease, British Empire–sponsored opium addiction, man-eating tigers and piracy on the seas. In 1887 interracial resentments led to riots.

By the 1930s and early 1940s, politics dominated the intellectual scene with the independence movement in India and communist struggles in China. Opposition to Japan's invasions of China in 1931 and 1937 was near universal in Singapore.

WWII & the Japanese Invasion

Singaporean Chinese were to pay a heavy price for opposing Japanese imperialism when General Yamashita Tomoyuki pushed his thinly stretched army into the undefended northwest of Singapore on 15 February 1942. For the British, who had established a vital naval base near the city in the 1920s, surrender was sudden and humiliating, and 140,000 Australian, British and oft-overlooked Indian troops were killed or imprisoned.

Japanese rule was harsh in Singapore, which was renamed Syonan (Light of the South). Yamashita herded up and interned the Europeans, many in the infamous Changi prison. Thousands of Chinese (Singapore claims 50,000, Japan says 6000) were targeted for torture and mass execution at Sentosa and Changi Beach. Malays and Indians were also subject to systematic abuse. Inflation skyrocketed, food, medicines and other essentials became scarce and starvation ensued.

The war ended suddenly with the atomic bombing of Nagasaki and Japan's surrender on 14 August 1945, and Singapore was passed back into British control. Despite an official apology in 1991 and generous monetary loans, Singapore has never forgotten, or forgiven the Japanese.

Singapore's tragic WWII history is commemorated in museums around the country.

Post-war Alienation

The British were welcomed back to Singapore but their right (and ability) to rule was now in question. Post-war poverty, unemployment and nationalist sentiment provided a groundswell of support for communism. Singapore moved slowly to self-government: the socialist Malayan Democratic Union was its first real political party, but it became increasingly radical and boycotted Singapore's first elections in 1947.

By the early 1950s the 'communist threat' had waned and left-wing activity was again on the upswing. One of the rising stars of this era was Lee Kuan Yew, a third-generation Straits-born Chinese who had studied law at Cambridge. The socialist People's Action Party (PAP) was founded in 1954 with Lee as secretary-general. A shrewd politician, Lee appealed for support to both the emerging British-educated elite and to radicalistic passions – the party included a communist faction and an ambitious post-Raffles plan of its own: strong state intervention to industrialise Singapore's economy.

Under arrangements for internal self-government, PAP won a majority of seats in the new Legislative Assembly in 1959, and Lee Kuan Yew became the first Singaporean prime minister – a title he held for the next 30 years.

Lee Kuan Yew

Under Lee's paternal reign of 30 years Singapore pursued an ambitious and highly successful program of defence, health, education, pension and housing schemes. Meanwhile political stability was ensured by exiling or jailing dissidents, banning critical publications and controlling public speech. In 1990 Lee Kuan Yew resigned in style following the completion of the Mass Rapid Transit (MRT) subway system – an impressive testament to Singapore's technological achievements – and the Republic of Singapore's grand 25th anniversary celebrations.

Movin' right along on the MRT: one of Lee Kuan Yew's many achievements.

Independent Singapore

By the early 1960s Britain had found a way to withdraw colonial rule in the region by creating the new state of Malaysia, uniting Malaya with Sabah, Sarawak and Singapore. Two years later in 1965 Singapore was expelled largely due to Malay fears of Chinese dominance. Singapore reluctantly struck out on its own and vigorously survived. Despite having no natural resources, under Lee Kuan Yew it quickly entrenched itself as Asia's financial centre and an 'economic miracle'.

ORIENTATION

Singapore is a city, an island and a country. Stamford Raffles founded Singapore on the Singapore River, which is still the heart of the city. To the south is the central business district centred on Raffles Place, and along the riverbanks are the popular renovated districts of Boat Quay and Clarke Quay. To the southwest Chinatown adjoins the CBD while to the north lies the colonial district. Farther north are Little India, based around Serangoon Rd, and Arab St, the Muslim centre of the city. From the colonial district, Bras Basah Rd heads northwest to become Orchard Rd, Singapore's main tourist area, with dozens of luxury hotels and shopping malls.

To the west of the island is the industrial area of Jurong, to the east the beachside East Coast district, to the northeast is Changi and the island of Pulau Ubin. Huge HDB (Housing & Development Board) high-rise blocks dominate the east and northeast. The central north and northwest is the least developed and is home to most of Singapore's remaining forest.

Finding Your Way

Addresses are often preceded by the number of the floor and then the shop or apartment number. Addresses do not quote the district or suburb. For example, #03-12 Far East Plaza, Scotts Rd is shop No 12 on the 3rd floor of the Far East Plaza.

Know where you're going if you want to get there...

ENVIRONMENT

Singapore stands out as an environmentally enlightened country in the region and enforces strict laws controlling littering and waste emissions – although until recently industry enjoyed a freer hand, and the litter patrol slacks off away from Orchard Rd. Development has left little of Singapore's wilderness, but growing interest in ecology and the public's desire for open space is urging the government towards conservation. You'll find primary and secondary rainforest around Bukit Timah Nature Reserve and mangrove forest on the northern coast and the offshore islands.

Singapore has a terrific Mass Rapid Transit (MRT) rail system and an extensive bus network. Good public transport coupled with prohibitive import duties, registration fees and licensing quotas restrict car ownership, resulting in remarkably pollution-free air. However, during bushfire season Singapore is plagued by clouds of smoke from forest fires in Indonesia and Malaysia. Like most countries Singapore is committed to conserving its environment but not at the expense of economic growth and prosperity.

GOVERNMENT & POLITICS

Singapore's government is based on the Westminster system. The unicameral parliament has 83 elected members representing 52 electoral divisions. Voting is compulsory. Governments are elected for five years, but a ruling government can dissolve parliament and call an election at any time.

As well as having elected members, the government has instituted a system that allows it to appoint an opposition. Nonconstituency Members of Parliament (NCMPs) are members who have failed to win enough votes, but are appointed to parliament as runners-up if fewer than four opposition members are elected. Singapore also has a popularly elected president but the position is largely ceremonial.

The legal system is also based on the British system with the Supreme Court as the ultimate arbitrator. The judiciary's independence is enshrined in the constitution, but many judges are appointed on short tenure and renewal is subject to party approval. Rulings that have gone against the government have seen new laws quickly enacted by parliament to ensure government victory.

Outspoken political opposition candidates are silenced by crippling defamation suits, jail sentences or being found guilty of 'tax evasion'.

ECONOMY

Singapore has no natural resources other than its harbour and well-educated population. Yet despite this, and despite its small size, it has become South-

Big harbour, big boats, big boxes, big bucks.

East Asia's most economically successful country. This prosperity is thanks to its location at the crossroads of international trade routes, its promotion of free trade and its attractiveness to foreign investors courtesy of generous tax breaks, few restrictions on the exchange of currency and excellent infrastructure.

Singapore has recorded a phenomenal growth rate averaging around 9% over the past 30 years. However, the Asian financial crisis in the mid-1990s followed by the post-11 September 2001 global slump plunged Singapore into its worst recession since 1967. Singapore's per capita GDP has fallen from US$26,000 in 1997 to around US$20,000.

Singapore's main industries include petroleum refining, electronics, oil-drilling equipment, rubber products, processed food and beverages, and financial services. In 2000, tourism contributed 22% of services exports. Singapore also has the highest rate of savings in the world – around US$60 billion – thanks to contributions to its compulsory pension scheme.

SOCIETY & CULTURE

Singapore is often portrayed by outsiders as a soulless money-making machine – an unkind assessment though not without some basis in fact. However, as prosperous Singapore forges ahead into the 21st century, it is keenly examining its own, unique identity and what it means to be Singaporean.

The government is keen to define the Singaporean identity, especially in its promotion of Asian values. Its neo-Confucian ideals are based on subservience to family and society, hard work and the desire to succeed. This dovetails neatly with the government's authoritarian notions of 'Asian democracy', which argue that Western pluralism and democracy are decadent luxuries that Singapore cannot afford. Unlike neighbouring Malaysia, Singapore promotes multiculturalism because the nation's economic success and the government's power monopoly are dependent on stable interracial relations (however, in general class terms the Chinese dominate the upper echelons while the Malays and Indians lag behind).

Many Singaporeans enjoy good education, access to health care and government-owned housing. In return they endure a barrage of government campaigns, sometimes enforced by law, which attempt to create conformity and cohesion at all costs. Programs range from banning nudity in the home, fines for

> **Did You Know?**
> - Singapore has as a teensy surface area of 1000 sq km
> - In a population of 4 million, overseas workers number 450,000
> - Singapore averages around one execution every nine days
> - The country's official languages are Malay, Mandarin, Tamil and English
> - Prime Minister Lee Kuan Yew nominated the air-conditioner as the most influential invention of the 20th century
> - Air-conditioners account for one-third of Singapore's electricity usage
> - In 2001 the ruling PAP government won another five-year term in a vote-less election thanks to insufficient numbers of opposition candidates

Pillars of the community at City Hall.

not flushing a public toilet and banning of chewing gum to courtesy campaigns, tax-breaks for well-educated mothers (ie, Chinese women) and the Filial Piety law which allowed parents to sue their kids for upkeep.

Freedom of speech and the press is limited and critiquing the government in a public forum can quickly land you in jail. Censorship is also an issue of interest especially given Singapore's current attempts to promote itself as an arts city. Despite Singapore's vibrant queer scene homosexuality is illegal – gay sex is punishable by a 10-year jail sentence and clubs are still subject to occasional crackdowns. Perhaps Singapore's greatest challenge now is to convince its youth – many of whom have enjoyed a lifetime of financial security – that all these restrictions are for the greater good.

Etiquette

Despite its hot and humid weather the standard of dress in Singapore is high. The better you dress the better you will be received.

Maintaining face is important across Asia, and Singapore is no exception – never lose your temper and remember that it's easier to solve disputes with a smile and a calm tone of voice.

Religion plays a major role in people's lives so treat it and devotees with respect. When visiting temples and shrines dress modestly and remove your shoes. Feet are considered unclean, so avoid pointing your foot at people and deities at Buddhist temples.

Passionate public kissing is frowned upon, but handholding is OK; you'll commonly see straight Indian men holding hands with their male friends.

Business Etiquette

Business cards are essential for doing business in Singapore. When exchanging business cards offer yours nameside up in a humble way using both hands with the card positioned between your thumbs. When receiving cards study the person's details with respectful attention and do not put the card away in the presence of the offeree.

Speak Good Singlish

The Singaporean government regularly runs campaigns promoting 'Speak Good English' and has actively discouraged the use of 'Singlish' in television and radio shows. But Singaporeans continue to revel in their local vernacular, a unique and often humorous mix of English – cut, clipped, reversed and revamped – and Malay and Hokkien Chinese words and expressions.

Singlish has some characteristics that can be mystifying for an English speaker, such as the fact that verb tenses are rarely used (eg, 'I go tomorrow' or 'I go yesterday'). Requests or questions are often marked with a tag ending, since direct questioning is considered rude. So, a question such as 'Would you like a beer?' might be rendered as 'You want beer or not?', which might come across to speakers of Western English as being extremely rude.

Some other Singlishisms are:

ah beng – unsophisticated, uneducated person with no fashion sense or style, who tends to believe social status depends on conspicuous accessories and who isn't nearly as cool as he thinks he is.
Can? – 'Is that OK?'
Can! – 'Yes! That's fine.'
chope – to reserve for oneself or friends, for example by putting a bag on a seat; often used by people who are *kiasu* (see p. 62).
lah – often tagged onto the end of sentences for emphasis: *No good, lah*, which could mean (among other things) 'I don't think that's such a good idea'.
steady lah – well done, excellent; an expression of praise.
switch-off – lazy; easy: *That job damn switch-off*.
ya ya – boastful, a show-off: *He always ya ya one*.

For more Singlish, see the Coxford Singlish Dictionary, compiled by satirical web gurus **e** www.talkingcock.com (meaning to talk nonsense) who are Singapore's most passionate champions of Singlish.

ARTS

Having proved itself as an economic power Singapore now wants to be seen as a smart and creative one too. When Goh Chok Tong took over the prime ministership from Lee Kuan Yew in 1990 one of his first acts was to create a Ministry of Arts. Fierce competition with Hong Kong's international arts festival (and resulting tourist dollars) has pushed the Singapore Arts Festival to get braver and more experimental, and with the opening of the US$500 million arts complex, Esplanade – Theatres on the Bay, the arts are set to become big business. Singapore hosts WOMAD annually – and since restrictions on dancing at public concerts were lifted things have really started to liven up!

Singaporean kids are subjected to enormous pressure (state and parental) to become economists, doctors or IT programmers and not waste their time playing sport or writing poetry. This means that some large-scale campaigning is required for Singaporeans to appreciate the value of the arts.

While local bands are yet to attract much attention, home-grown theatre groups are pushing the boundaries with performances of local and international works with a Singaporean twist. Likewise, the visual and digital arts are gearing up for a more prominent role in Singapore's cultural life. Singapore's arts scene may be a babe in the woods, but it's already showing its teeth.

The Writing on the Wall

In 1994 US teenager Michael Fay created an international incident when, despite then US president Bill Clinton's plea for clemency, his brattish graffiti spree in Singapore landed him in prison with six lashes of the rotan. Today, would-be taggers can work their magic at Singapore's government-run skateboard park, off Orchard Rd. However, only 'healthy, creative expression' is allowed; works are regularly inspected and any material considered offensive is promptly removed.

Street art: keep it kosher or you could be whipped into shape.

Feel like somebody's watching? Movie posters adorn walls around town.

Chinese Opera

In Singapore *wayang*, or Chinese opera, stems from the vaudeville-like Cantonese tradition. What it lacks in literary nuance is made up for by garish costumes, and the crashing music that follows the action. Performances can go for an entire evening and it is usually easy for the uninitiated to follow the gist of the action. The acting is very stylised, and the music can be searing to Western ears, but seeing a performance is a worthwhile experience. Street and HDB block performances are held during important festivals such as Chinese New Year, the Festival of the Hungry Ghosts and the Festival of the Nine Emperor Gods.

Film

Singapore's film production industry has experienced a strong revival since its slump in the 1980s and the annual Singapore Film Festival is helping to build Singaporeans' taste for fine international film. In 1998 the Singapore Film Commission was established to 'nurture, support and promote' Singaporean talent in the film industry, however, scissor-happy censors don't exactly make things easy.

In 1995 a new RA rating was created (Restricted Artistic, to be shown only in specially licensed inner-city theatres and only to people 21 years and over). *Bugis Street* was the first to take advantage of the rating and slipped past the censors virtually cut-free. Notable Singaporean films include: Eric Khoo's *Mee Pok Man* and *12 Storeys,* a gritty depiction of a life in an HDB housing block; Tay Teck Lock's *Money No Enough* and Glen Goei's disco hit *Forever Fever*. Other favourites are *Army Daze*, a comedy about military service, *I Not Stupid,* a poignant comedy about how Singapore's education system can have tragic consequences for non-conforming individuals, and the satirical comedy hit *Talking Cock*.

Glamour, glitter and greasepaint: Chinese opera, Singapore-style.

highlights

The best thing about Singapore is its surprising and unique weirdness. You might find yourself sweating over a spicy laksa surrounded by cool, suited Singaporean businessmen who can simultaneously SMS text, clinch a deal and wield a pair of chopsticks faster than Zorro can whip off his mask; or spice shopping in Little India and feeling the need to break into song and dance and re-enact your own Bollywood fantasy; or racing a mountain bike helter-skelter through the jungle of Pulau Ubin and having to suddenly swerve to avoid a chicken. Singapore doesn't have the messy human chaos of Bangkok, the high-tech freneticness of Tokyo or the grand outdoors of Sydney, but it does have all these things in small, Singaporean-sized pieces.

Stopping Over?

One Day Spend the morning wandering around Chinatown and sampling its culinary wonders; then head to the World Trade Centre (WTC) and cable car your way up Mt Faber for a view of the city and a beer at Altivo; then while away the evening with a leisurely stroll along the Quay and dinner at Empress Place.

Two Days Wander around the Padang and visit the Asian Civilisations Museum, then take in a typical lunch at Armenian Kopitiam or Killiney Rd before bracing yourself for some Orchard Rd shopping action and dinner on trendy Club St.

Three Days Spend the morning exploring Little India then chill out at the Botanic Gardens, building up an appetite for a pepper crab feast at Newton Food Centre, followed by a show at the Esplanade or some disco action at Zouk.

Singapore Lowlights

Driving is a pain, Orchard Rd is crowded with horrible transnational franchises and we really wish the government would stop transforming its authentic attractions – both cultural and natural – into sanitised Disney versions of their true selves.

Un-happy snaps: 'I could be anyhere in the world' logos.

ASIAN CIVILISATIONS MUSEUM   (3, K6)

Built in 1865, the imposing Empress Place building was named in honour of Queen Victoria and underwent various incarnations before the STB (Singapore Tourism Board) turned it into a Chinese museum in 1988. In 1992 it was declared a national monument and was incorporated into the government's strategy for revamping and reviving Singapore's cultural life.

INFORMATION

- ✉ 1 Empress Pl
- ☎ 6332 2982
- e www.museum.org.sg
- Ⓜ Raffles Place
- 🕐 Tues-Sun 9am-6pm (Fri to 9pm)
- $ $3/1
- ⓘ on-site information counter
- ♿ good
- ✗ Siem Reap II

In 2002 the new branch of the Asian Civilisations Museum opened its doors, leaving the Singapore History Museum for dead, with its swish, renovated interior and sophisticated exhibits. The museum hosts regular touring and programmed exhibitions in addition to its five galleries dedicated to exploring different aspects of cultural life in Asia. The South-East Asia gallery explores the region's diversity and the interconnections between Hinduism, Buddhism and Islam and their respective ethnic and cultural groups. The East Asia gallery focuses on China and the West gallery on the world of Islam, while the South Asia gallery traces Hinduism, Buddhism and Jainism through the Indian and Sri Lankan traditions. The final gallery examines Singapore's mercantile history in the context of the Singapore River. This is probably the best way to get a handle on Singapore's historic development and see how it relates to the region, and in turn, how Singaporeans relate – or don't relate – to each other.

The Asian Civilisations Museum branch at Armenian St (see p. 39) offers complementary exhibits.

The rich textures of Asia.

DON'T MISS
- 8th-century Koran fragment written in Kufic
- five-metre-long Tibetan silk *thangka* (prayer cloth)

BUKIT TIMAH NATURE RESERVE   (2, E6)

Go troppo in Bukit Timah Nature Reserve where it's hard to believe you're in Singapore. This 81-hectare reserve is all that's left of Singapore's once bountiful forests. It is said to host more plant species than the entire North American continent and provides a much needed refuge to what remains of Singapore's wildlife, including flying lemurs, pythons and birds such as the racquet-tailed drongo and white-bellied sea eagle. However as a visitor you are most likely to see long-tailed macaques, squirrels and mosquitoes. The reserve also boasts the highest point in Singapore, 162m Bukit Timah.

There are several well-established and signposted trails which are popular with walkers and mountain bikers. The best **trails for spotting wildlife** explore the forest and run off the summit road. Try the North View, South View or Fern Valley paths; these involve

INFORMATION

- ✉ 177 Hindhede Dr
- ☎ 1800 468 5736
- 🚌 TIBS 171 from
  Ⓜ Newton
- ⏱ 7am-7pm
- 💲 free
- ⓘ Visitor Centre
  8.30am-6pm
- ✕ drinks only at kiosk

Feathered & Furry Friends

Although they are now believed to be extinct on the island, tigers, clouded leopards and mouse deer all once inhabited Singapore. Today the most common animals are long-tailed macaques (grey-brown monkeys) and squirrels. Singapore is also home to the reticulated python, which grows up to 10m in length, the poisonous pit viper and over 300 bird species.

some scrambling over rocks and tree roots, but are easily negotiated.

Some of the walks are quite strenuous so bring plenty of water and sun protection – it's also hot and humid so try to time your visit for the cooler part of the day.

Monkey business: no feeding allowed.

Bukit Timah has two well-surfaced **mountain-bike trails**, 7km in all, which cut though jungle and abandoned quarry sites.

Remember to be sensitive to the environs – don't leave litter lying around and don't feed the animals – it's bad for their diet and creates bad habits.

CHANGI MUSEUM & CHAPEL   (2, E13)

Built in commemoration of the Allied Changi POWs who were captured, imprisoned and suffered horrific treatment at the hands of the invading Japanese forces during WWII; the museum was shifted from the original Changi prison site when Singapore Prisons recently reclaimed the land to expand its operations.

INFORMATION

✉ 1000 Upper Changi
    Rd North
☎ 6214 2451
🚇 2 from Ⓜ Tanah
    Merah
🕐 9.30am-4.30pm
⑤ free
ⓘ call for guided tours
♿ good

Changi Museum, a sombre remembrance.

The Singapore Tourist Bureau (STB) raised the funds for this venture which is now run by private contractors. Former POWs, veterans and historians will feel the loss of the actual site most keenly.

The museum project architects won an award by default (no opposing nominations) but to their credit the understated design is more suited to the museum's dual shrine/historical role than architectural high drama. The square white facade is reminiscent of a concrete bunker, yet the planted greenery hints at healing and renewal while the gaping entrance and open plan suggest accessibility and transparency.

The museum centrepiece is a replica of the original **Changi chapel** built by inmates as a focus for worship and presumably as a sign of solidarity and strength. Services are held on Sundays but the shadeless courtyard heats up like an oven and the sun is too bright to bear. In stark contrast is the **Voices of Changi** exhibit housed in a long, narrow black cell with voice-over reminiscences by ex-POWs and nurses. Not recommended for claustrophobics or anyone having trauma flashbacks.

In keeping with the memorial theme the exhibit is strictly low-key; the story is told quietly and poignantly through photographs, artefacts and survivors' testimonials – bring tissues.

DON'T MISS

- war art exhibition
- remembrances pinned to the chapel notice board

CHINATOWN   (3, L4)

Singapore's cultural heart is Chinatown. Roughly bounded by the Singapore River to the north, New Bridge Rd to the west, Maxwell Rd to the south and Cecil St to the east, it provides a glimpse of the old ways, and how the Chinese immigrants who shaped and built modern Singapore used to live.

The first immigrants arrived by junk from China in 1821 – it was they who built the **Thian Hock Keng Temple** (see p. 36) in thanks

INFORMATION

Ⓜ Raffles Place, Outram Park, Tanjong Pagar
✗ see pp. 75-7

to the goddess of the sea for a safe journey. For those settlers seeking a new life the reality was a shock: hard working conditions, poor sanitation, disease, poverty, homesickness and opium addiction marked the early years.

Much of Chinatown has been torn down and redeveloped over the past 30 years, though the greatest changes have occurred in the last decade. Chinatown used to enjoy sea breezes until land reclamation shunted it a few blocks inland. Many of the old colonial shopfronts were bulldozed until the Urban Redevelopment Authority (URA) realised with a start there were very few left. They then began restoring them, or rather gutting them and restoring or rebuilding their facades in the same style. Entire strips have been saved and painted in bright tourist-friendly colours. Some traditional businesses have given way to souvenir shops and upmarket restaurants.

Nonetheless Chinatown is an interesting and vibrant place to be, from the Chinatown Complex wet market and dusty medical halls to traditional bakeries, mah jong clubs and chic bars.

Chinatown's streets come alive at night.

DON'T MISS
• night-time hawker stalls • traditional teahouses and kick-ass Chinese coffee • Al-Abrar Mosque • Thian Hock Keng Temple (see p. 36) • Sri Mariamman Temple (see p. 35)

ESPLANADE – THEATRES ON THE BAY (3, J7)

Designed to resemble an old-fashioned microphone, the surreal Esplanade arts development has been referred to as fly's eyes, a honeycomb, two upturned durians and a whole lot of rude words we can't repeat here. Whether you love it or lump it the brand new Esplanade (designed by UK outfit Michael Wilford and Partners and local DP Architects) will become an icon of Singapore like Sydney's Opera House or Bilbao's Guggenheim Museum. The design also makes a dramatic contrast with its colonial surrounds.

Built on reclaimed land along the waterfront the $600 million Esplanade project has been in the pipeline since the 1970s, but wasn't commissioned until 1993. It took two years to prepare the land just to be able to support the structure; reclaimed land is created by building up and compacting sand and silt. Then, strangely, the building was built from the inside out. The controversial exterior is made from variously angled aluminium shades that maximise the natural light while shielding the glass roof from the sun; by night internal lighting sets the building aglow. Amazingly the entire structure rests upon an enormous rubber slab, so if a giant King Kong goes on a Singaporean rampage he'll be able to pick the whole thing up and eat it in one gulp.

The complex houses a 1600-seat concert hall featuring US sound designer Russell Johnson's trademark acoustic canopy (a big, swirly, wooden structure dominating the ceiling that can be lowered to maximise sound quality) and a super-duper 4,889-pipe Klais organ; plus a 2000-seat horseshoe theatre, smaller studios, art galleries, outdoor performance spaces and a library devoted to the performing arts. A three-storey mall houses restaurants, bars and arty boutiques.

Local independent arts groups view the Esplanade with mixed feelings. On one hand the Esplanade will raise the profile of the arts locally, provide opportunities for international collaborations, and hopefully help

INFORMATION

- ✉ 60 Raffles Ave
- ☎ 6337 3711
- e www.esplanade.com
- Ⓜ City Hall
- 🚌 7, 97, 124, 167, 174
- 🕐 arts centre: 7am-late; box office 10am-9pm; mall: 11am-9.30pm; restaurants, cafes & bars: 11am-late
- ⑤ free entry; variable ticket prices for shows
- ⓘ information centre on site
- ♿ good
- ✗ on-site mall

Esplanade Theatres: distinctive roof detail.

enliven Singapore's emerging arts scene. On the other hand the large concert spaces and huge rental costs mean that it's unlikely that many local arts groups – most of whom are non-profit – will ever be able to access the Esplanade's state-of-the-art facilities, and may find themselves swamped by the complex's superior resources and exhaustive marketing for international blockbusters. Either way it will be interesting to see how the Esplanade handles issues such as censorship – will it help push the boundaries or simply toe the line? Further, with Singapore struggling through a recession will the city be able to support the new venture, or will the Esplanade start to smell like a big, durian-scented folly?

For the visitor, however, the Esplanade is good news. Even if you don't want to take in a show a steady stream of free outdoor performances should keep you entertained. And as Lee Weng Choy, director of the alternative art complex Substation, was quoted in *I-S Magazine*: 'Even if the place is disappointing in terms of programming the seats at least should be comfortable.'

Don't Give Up Your Day Job

Until recently busking was illegal in Singapore – being viewed as a sneaky form of begging rather than a form of artistic expression. Today punters can enjoy an annual Singapore River Buskers Festival. Singaporeans are even allowed to busk providing that they audition and obtain approval for a three-month licence and donate their earnings (after expenses) to charity.

The fly's eyes or the bee's knees?

FORT CANNING (3, H4)

When Raffles rocked into Singapore and claimed it for the mother country, locals were fearful of climbing the sacred place Bukit Larangan (Forbidden Hill) out of respect for the shrine of Sultan Iskander Shah, the last ruler of the ancient kingdom of Singapura. Demonstrating the brand of cultural sensitivity that characterised colonial rule, Raffles promptly cleared the jungle – thus uncovering Javanese artefacts from the 14th-century Majapahit empire – and finding the resulting view to his liking decided to build himself a house. The area was known as Government House until the military built Fort Canning in 1860.

INFORMATION

⊠ Cox Terrace
☎ 6332 1200, 1800 4717 300
e www.nparks.gov.sg
Ⓜ Dhoby Ghaut
⑤ free
♿ OK
✗ Cafe at-sunrice

Today **Fort Canning Park** acts as green lung for the populace – providing a space for peace and respite and a much needed habitat for birds such as black-naped orioles and collared kingfishers. Atop the hill you'll find the *keramat* (sacred shrine) underneath a 14th-century-style Malay roof. Despite signage strictly banning any kinds of religious activity here, the shrine remains a popular spot for private prayer for all Singaporeans, regardless of religion. Even today the shrine is regarded as a focal point for ancestral spirits. The shrine usually bears small offerings such as jasmine garlands – treat the site with respect and consider removing your shoes if you step up on the platform.

Fort Canning's historic cannon guards tranquil parkland and a sacred shrine.

Fort Canning is also home to the fine **Battle Box** museum (see p. 39) and hosts cultural activities ranging from WOMAD and Ballet Under the Stars to performances at its Black Box theatre. Check the website or street press for details. You can also tour the Spice Garden and take cooking classes at the **Academy at-sunrice** (see p. 61).

DON'T MISS
• poignant tombstones of early settlers • ASEAN sculpture garden
• scenic lookout

JURONG BIRD PARK   (2, F4)

If you're the kind of person who likes nothing better than to rise at dawn and lurk amid the reeds with a pair of binoculars pressed to your eyes and a copy of *What Bird is That* by your side then this is the place for you. But even if you find our feathered friends dull and perhaps a little stupid (what's so hard about the concept of 'glass window'?) Jurong Bird Park still makes a pleasant escape from the hustle and bustle of downtown.

Built to provide Singaporeans with a nature escape, Jurong is one of the largest bird parks in the region (over 20 hectares) and is home to around 8000 birds, representing around 600 species, about 30 of them endangered. It specialises in South-East Asian and tropical species though there are also around 200 penguins living in Arctic conditions at the **Penguin Parade**. The walk-in **Waterfall Aviary** is the park's highlight; it houses 1500 birds who are free to fly within the interior and splash in their very own 30m-high custom-made waterfall.

There are various shows and bird-feeding displays throughout the day; highlights include Birds of Prey (10am and 4pm daily) and the All Star Bird Show (11am and 3pm) featuring cockatoos, macaws and toucans playing with ping-pong balls, flying through hoops and singing 'Happy Birthday'. It's not exactly educational but it's entertaining – especially for kids.

The site is well-treed with plenty of comfort stops along the way so it makes for a cool and breezy outing – if you're feeling especially lazy you can take in the park from the panorail.

The park sometimes promotes cheap admission and 'Breakfast with the Birds' deals – inquire by phone.

INFORMATION

- ✉ 2 Jurong Hill
- ☎ 6265 0022
- e www.birdpark.com.sg
- 🚌 SBS 194, 251 from Ⓜ Boon Lay
- ⏲ 8am-6pm
- ⑂ $12/5; panorail $3/2
- ⓘ information counter at entrance
- ♿ good
- ✕ cafes & restaurants throughout the park

An All Star Bird getting cocky.

DON'T MISS
- Breakfast with the Birds • simulated thunderstorm in the South-East Asian Aviary (noon) • new Rainbow Aviary and tree house (opens 2003)

LITTLE INDIA   (3, C8)

Little India is a world apart from the rest of Singapore. Originally a European enclave, the neighbourhood evolved into an Indian cultural centre after a Jewish Indian businessman started farming buffalo here. Today Little India remains true to its heritage: incense sticks and henna dyes jostle for space with spices, jasmine garlands, gold thread saris, wildly coloured milk sweets and pumping Bollyrock direct from the latest musical blockbuster.

INFORMATION

Ⓜ Bugis
🚌 65, 97, 103, 106, 139
✕ see pp. 84-5

You'll see tourist groups passing through on rickshaws or on tours but this is a fairly uncool way to experience the Little India vibe. Highlights to explore on your own include the **Tekka Centre** market where you'll find deliciously flaky *roti prata*, decorative brass wear and dripping slabs of bloody meat all crammed into the one treasure trove/little shop of horrors. The **Little India Arcade** is touristy but good for souvenirs. Clive St and Campbell Lane boast astrologers, traditional beauty treatments, bangles and trinkets of all kinds. Kerbau Rd is taking off as an arts haven with religious art shops, art galleries and two theatre groups. Oh, and did we mention food? A mere $2 will send you directly to curry heaven.

These days Little India is populated chiefly by men on two-year contracts from India, Bangladesh and Sri Lanka doing all the dirty jobs that Singaporeans aren't keen on. The wildest time to visit is Sunday evening when around 10,000 of these guys celebrate their day off and hang out gossiping, shopping and going to the Sri Veeramakaliamman Temple. Solo women travellers may find the crowds a little intimidating.

Fabulous fakery: adorn yourself with riches in the streets of Little India.

DON'T MISS

• temples • cups of ginger tea • sari shops • Sri Lankan curries • Sunday nights

MT FABER (2, H8)

On the southern side of the city opposite the World Trade Centre (WTC) and not far from Sentosa Island is Mt Faber which, standing proud if not tall at 105m, provides one of the best views in Singapore. Take the cable car to the top ($8.50/3.90) or begin the steep climb from the bottom where you'll catch glimpses of old colonial **black and white houses** and the strikingly stripy **Danish Seaman's Mission** building.

INFORMATION

- ⊠ Mt Faber
- 🚌 from WTC, after
- 🚌 61, 97, 124, 143, 166
- Ⓢ free
- ✕ Altivo (see p. 93)

The park is steeply terraced so there's not much room for lolling around off the paths, but there are a number of well-positioned benches which provide shady reading spaces. Look out for bougainvillea, red flame trees and other tropical greenery.

Kampong Life

Fifty years ago the view from Mt Faber would have been vastly different. Up until the 1950s most Singaporeans were living in simple single-storey homes in kampongs (traditional Malay villages) where everyone knew everyone's business and kids and chickens roamed free. However, population pressures and land scarcity meant that neighbourly comforts were eventually sacrificed to provide housing solutions. While Singaporeans remain sentimental about those kampong days, today 90% of the population lives in government-built high-rise flats – a phenomenal achievement.

From the summit you'll see Singapore in all its strange splendour. To the south is the port, the sea, giant cranes and sinister-looking columns of smoke pumping into the sky, while to the north lies a skyscape of high-rise Housing Development Board housing blocks which teeter as far as the park's edge. To the east of the cable-car station is the seaside themed **Marina Deck** lookout, which has all the hallmarks of a tourist attraction gone wrong – but the views are free.

Singapore's *Cosmo* magazine recently voted Mt Faber's Altivo lounge bar one of the best spots for after-dark hanky-panky...

In the mood for altitude? Mt Faber's Altivo bar.

ORCHARD ROAD   (4)

Orchard Rd is a living shrine to the power of capitalism, globalisation and the modern belief that you are what you buy – the route to nirvana is via a marked-down pair of designer shoes. Of course, it's not a bad place for shopping either – one of Singapore's top pastimes.

INFORMATION

- ✉ Orchard Rd
- Ⓜ Orchard, Somerset, Dhoby Ghaut
- ♿ difficult due to pedestrians
- ✕ see pp. 80-2

Orchard Rd: I shop therefore I am.

In the 19th century this stretch of road was literally an orchard lined with nutmeg and pepper plantations, traffic was strictly pedestrian and evening strolls were marred by the odd flood. These days Orchard Rd is lined with mega-sized malls, five-star hotels and transnational franchises with only a few nearby hints of former times: the Germanic inspired **Goodwood Park Hotel** (3, C1) on Scotts Rd, which dates from 1900; the President's **Istana** (palace; 3, D3), which formerly housed British governors; a strip of dodgy restaurants in old shophouses along **Cuppage Terrace** (4, B9); and the pleasant strip of shophouses along **Emerald Hill Rd**.

Hectic at the best of times, Orchard Rd explodes into high-density mayhem on the weekends when Singaporeans flock in to shop and use the strip like an extended loungeroom. There's not much space or privacy in an HDB flat so it's a hot spot for youngsters and couples to hang out, gossip, compare mobile phone dial tones and indulge in some low-key canoodling away from parental eyes.

Orchard Rd offers one of the world's densest shopping experiences. To survive you'll need comfortable shoes, sharp elbows and a gold credit card. Despite the constant sales it's not a bargain hunter's paradise – luckily window-shopping is free.

DON'T MISS
- Louis Vuitton shop window ● 40,000 sq ft of books at Kinokuniya, Ngee Ann City ● popular local eats on Killiney Rd (4, D9)

THE PADANG (3, J7)

There is no more obvious a symbol of British colonialism than the open field of the Padang. It is here that flannelled fools played cricket in the tropical heat, cheered on by the Singapore Cricket Club members in the pavilion. At the opposite end of the field is the Singapore Recreation Club, which was set aside for the Eurasian community. Cricket is still played on the weekends but segregation is, officially, no longer practised.

The Padang was a centre for colonial life and a place to promenade in the evenings. The neighbouring Esplanade Park on the foreshore is still a nice spot for an evening stroll. The Padang also witnessed the beginning of the end of colonial rule, for it was here that the invading Japanese herded the European community together, before marching them off to Changi prison.

INFORMATION

- ✉ The Padang
- Ⓜ City Hall
- ♿ good
- ✗ Empress Place eateries

Nonya & Baba

Singapore's Padang-promenading colonists found friends among the Peranakan community – Singaporean-born Chinese families whose distinct culture combined Chinese and Malay traditions. Peranakan women were known as Nonya, the men as Baba – you'll see these names used in some of the city's traditional Peranakan restaurants. 'Peranakan', which means 'half-caste', wasn't always a flattering term but today Singapore's best museums all pay nostalgic homage to this ethnic group.

The Padang is ringed by imposing colonial buildings. The **Victoria Theatre & Concert Hall** (1862) was once the town hall. It is now used for cultural events and is the home of the Singapore Symphony Orchestra. **Parliament House** (1827) is Singapore's oldest government building. High St, which runs next to Parliament House, was hacked from the jungle to become Singapore's first street, and was an Indian area in its early days. The **Supreme Court and City Hall**, where Lord Louis Mountbatten accepted the Japanese surrender in 1945, are two other stoic colonial buildings, on St Andrew's Rd. Built in 1939, the Supreme Court is a relatively new addition, and was the last classical building to be erected in Singapore.

Colonial grandeur: The Victoria Theatre & Concert Hall.

PULAU UBIN (2, C13)

Legend has it that an unlikely trio of a frog, an elephant and a boar challenged one another to a swimming race across the Johor Strait. The first to fail was the frog who was transformed into the diminutive Pulau Sekudu; soon the boar and the elephant also tired and the two were transformed into Pulau Ubin. Non-athletic visitors will be relieved to know that these days the trip to the island from Changi jetty merely takes a chugging 15mins by rustic and oil-smoking 'bumboat'.

INFORMATION

- ☎ 6542 4108, office 6542 4842
- **e** www.nparks.gov.sg
- 🚌 2 from Ⓜ Tanah Merah, followed by boat from Changi Village Jetty
- Ⓢ free
- ⓘ ranger station at jetty
- ✕ pier-side cafes

Pulau Ubin: best seen on two wheels.

Historically the first settlers are believed to have been Indonesian dissidents who arrived by boat in the late 1800s, established their community and built a mosque some decades later.

Singaporeans like to wax nostalgic about Pulau Ubin's kampong (village) atmosphere which seems a world apart. Not so sentimental are the folks who reportedly bulldozed the aforementioned mosque and plan the relocation of those settlers' direct descendents to highrises on the mainland. It's only a matter of time before the island becomes another Sentosa, so visit sooner, not later.

The island itself is a pleasant expanse of hilly greenery and the pace is lazy. Battered taxis wait by the pier while the drivers chew the fat in a straw-eating kind of way, chickens squawk and hot dogs slump where they stand.

The best way to get around is by hiring a mountain bike ($5-10 a day) which coincidentally is also about the only thing to do. On weekends the island is overrun with couples, teenagers and ex-pat families taking to the paths with gusto, mopping their sweating brows and sucking on cold coconut drinks. You can swim and camp at Noordin beach, but it's small and a little grotty; due to drownings, swimming in the quarries is no longer allowed (fine $1000) so sadly you're unlikely to swim in anything but your own sweat. Note that tap water on Pulau Ubin is not drinkable, so bring your own supply, or buy it at the pier.

The park runs occasional botanic and sea-creature tours – call for dates.

DON'T MISS • Thai Temple • Ubin Seafood Restaurant (☎ 6545 8202)

RAFFLES HOTEL (3, H7)

It's one of the world's most hyped hotels but no matter how you look at it – there's only one Raffles. While some countries are all too eager to leave their colonial past behind, Raffles is a much loved Singapore institution and an architectural landmark that has been classified by the government as part of the nation's 'cultural heritage'.

Raffles was opened in 1887 by the Sarkies brothers, immigrants from Armenia who are also associated with two other grand colonial hotels, the Strand in Yangon (Rangoon) and the Eastern & Oriental in Penang.

Raffles Hotel started life as a 10-room bungalow, but its heyday began with the opening of the main building in 1899. Raffles soon became a byword for Oriental luxury and attracted colonial literary giants such as Joseph Conrad, Somerset Maugham, Rudyard Kipling and Noel Coward. Other claims to fame include the fabled last Singaporean tiger shooting, in the Billiard Room in 1902, and the invention of the Singapore Sling by bartender Ngiam Tong Boon in 1915.

The fine frolics were put to an abrupt end when the Japanese invaded during WWII and started demanding room service. After the war the hotel became a transit camp for liberated Allied prisoners, by which time the glamour days were well and truly over.

INFORMATION

- ✉ 1 Beach Rd
- ☎ 6337 1886
- e www.raffleshotel.com
- Ⓜ City Hall
- Ⓢ free
- ♿ good
- ✕ throughout

Raffles Hotel – no place for riffraff.

Raffles was narrowly saved from the demolition ball in 1987 when the government declared it a protected monument. A $160 million face-lift ensued, complete with upmarket shopping mall, museum and Raffles souvenir shop. Stop by to admire the grounds or indulge in a Sunday brunch or high tea.

DON'T MISS • Raffles Hotel Museum (3rd floor, 9am-10pm) • throwing peanut shells on the floor and drinking Singapore Slings in the Long Bar

SENTOSA ISLAND   (1)

One person's highlight is another's lowlight – in the case of Sentosa Island it somehow manages to be both. The Brits turned this tiny island at the southern tip of Singapore into a military fortress in the late 1800s. In 1967 the island was returned to the government who developed it into a holiday resort. Military barracks transformed into 'vacation chalets', the fort became a museum complete with a merry tourist 'train', camouflage was officially out and bikinis were in.

The Sentosa philosophy is that too much is never enough. Already the island is covered in a bewildering array of attractions – ranging from the absurd psuedo-Mayan **Volcano Land** complete with tribal dancers from Malaysian Sabah to the **Musical Fountain**, which projects visitors' love messages onto a waterscreen. However, there are no signs that the development has abated.

The best way to enjoy Sentosa is to embrace its garishness and hit the attractions with a vengeance. **Underwater World** and the **Images of Singapore** museum are recommended. Alternatively swear off the commercial attrac-

INFORMATION

- ✉ Sentosa Island
- ☎ 1800 736 8672, emergency/ranger 6279 1155
- **e** www.sentosa.com.sg
- 🚌 Sentosa Service A from Seah Im Bus Terminal (opposite World Trade Centre), E from Orchard Rd, C from Ⓜ Tiong Bahru
- 🚟 from World Trade Centre, 8.30am-9pm ($8.50/3.90)
- ⛴ from World Trade Centre Domestic Ferry Terminal, 9.30am-10pm
- Ⓢ $6/4 or $12/6 per vehicle of five people before 5pm/after 9pm; includes free transport on the island but not entry to attractions
- ⓘ information counter at ferry terminal (8.30am-5.30pm)
- ♿ OK
- 🍴 restaurants or cafes at all attractions

tions and stick to nature: head to **Central Beach** for a dip, take the **Dragon Trail Nature Walk** or hire a mountain bike and explore the island with a picnic lunch.

You can also play volleyball, go horse riding, play soccer and golf or hire a kayak. Keep in mind though that this is Singapore so the weather is hot and sticky.

Sentosa Nights

For some frisky high jinks in the fresh air Sentosa hosts monthly **Black Moon Foam Parties** and **ZoukOut**, Singapore's annual outdoor rave. For details check local street press or the Sentosa website.

SINGAPORE ART MUSEUM (3, G6)

Opened in 1996, the Singapore Art Museum is the first of a series of national museums developed by the National Heritage Board. It is housed in a classical baroque-style building dating from 1867, formerly home to St Joseph's Catholic boys school. Rather than bulldozing it when the school relocated in 1987 local architect Wong Hooe Wai was commissioned to preserve, renovate and reconstruct the edifice into a modern art gallery. The result is an attractive design that fuses historical charm with a strong contemporary feel. Features include Filipino artist Ramon Orlina's **abstract glass window** in the former school chapel and US artist Dale Chihuly's sea anemone-like **blown-glass installations**.

The gallery focuses on Singaporean and regional artists with exhibitions ranging from classical Chinese calligraphy to contemporary works examining issues of Asian identity and the modern Singaporean experience. This makes for exciting, challenging programming

INFORMATION

- ✉ 71 Bras Basah Rd
- ☎ 6332 3222
- e www.nhb.gov.sg /SAM/sam.shtml
- Ⓜ City Hall
- ◷ Tues-Sun 9am-6pm (Fri to 9pm)
- ⓢ $3/1.50/8; free entry Fri 6pm-9pm
- ⓘ information desk; guided tours in English: Mon-Fri 11am & 2pm, Sat-Sun 11am, 2pm & 3.30pm; Japanese: Mon-Sun 10.30am
- ♿ good
- ✗ Dome (see p. 78), Paladino (see p. 79)

Cruise the classical courtyard at the Singapore Art Museum.

Keep Your Shirt On

In 1994 performance artist Josef Ng was banned from performing and fined for 'committing obscene acts', namely exposing his buttocks and snipping his pubic hair during a New Year's performance to protest against the arrest of 12 homosexuals. The resulting publicity and public hysteria led to the government officially retracting funding for performance art and other unscripted works on the grounds that those genres posed 'greater risks to public order, security and decency'.

complemented by touring exhibits. There's also a strong emphasis on the electronic arts movement, which has exploded in nearby Japan, China and Malaysia.

In addition to collecting and exhibiting, the gallery has a mission to bring a higher profile to the arts in Singapore and promote their value to a state which until now has focused on economic aims. In this respect the gallery fosters dialogue about Singaporean history and culture and how the nation might evolve in the future.

SINGAPORE BOTANIC GARDENS (2, F8)

Wide green spaces are few and far between in Singapore, which is why you can't beat the Botanic Gardens as a spot to unwind and recover from your jet lag, read a paper, picnic or just lie around daydreaming.

Established around 1860 and covering 52 hectares, the gardens are a legacy of British colonials whose penchant for collecting and displaying plants and artefacts for 'scientific' purposes was unparalleled. Originally the gardens acted as a testing point for potential cash crops – such as rubber – and botanical research. Today they host a herbarium housing more than 600,000 botanical specimens, and a library with archival materials dating back to the 16th century.

Travellers can enjoy manicured garden beds or explore a four-hectare patch of 'original Singaporean jungle', a small sample of the kind of forest that once covered the entire island.

The gardens are also home to the **National Orchid Garden**, one of the world's largest orchid displays featuring over 60,000 plants. Hype aside, orchids are extraordinary looking little things and are worth a look even if you don't really dig flowers.

At the time of writing the gardens were preparing for future developments including an educational

INFORMATION

- ✉ Cluny Rd
- ☎ 6471 7361
- e www.nparks.gov.sg
- 🚌 7, 77, 106, 123, 174
- ⏲ 5am-midnight; National Orchid Garden: 8.30am-7pm
- 💲 free; National Orchid Garden $2/1
- ⓘ information desk at entrance; call to arrange tours
- ♿ good
- ✗ Café Les Amis (see p. 88), Halia (see p. 89), Au Jardin Les Amis (see p. 88)

Orchids: a national pride and joy.

Children's Garden, an Evolution Garden and a 'Cool House' – the opposite of a hothouse – which will house South-East Asian plants from milder climes and high elevations.

The gardens also host free open-air music concerts on Sunday evenings for most of the year – call the garden or check with the Singapore Tourism Board (STB) for details.

Orchids

Singapore's national flower is the Vanda Miss Joaquim orchid and orchid displays are ubiquitous in the nation's hotel lobbies. Singapore is one of the best places to view a sampling of 30,000 species of orchids and 100,000 hybrids. With their delicate stems and petals, orchids seem like the classic fragile flower but they're actually one of the world's toughest species, capable of flourishing in climes ranging from desert to rainforest.

SINGAPORE SCIENCE CENTRE   (2, F5)

The Science Centre is a great spot for kids and not bad entertainment for adults either. This sprawling complex boasts exhibits galore ranging from one-button-wonders to exhaustive (and not so entertaining) displays on biotechnology. The mission is to educate in an informal and amusing way – admittedly most of the learning is probably by default but the kids don't seem to mind.

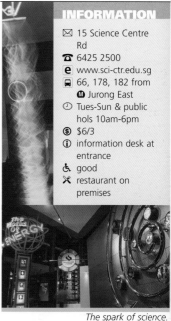

INFORMATION

- ✉ 15 Science Centre Rd
- ☎ 6425 2500
- ⒠ www.sci-ctr.edu.sg
- 🚌 66, 178, 182 from Ⓜ Jurong East
- 🕐 Tues-Sun & public hols 10am-6pm
- ⓢ $6/3
- ⓘ information desk at entrance
- ♿ good
- ✗ restaurant on premises

The spark of science.

Singapore Swill

Singapore has no natural water resources of its own, and has always relied on neighbouring Malaysia and Indonesia to provide it with drinking water. This dependence means that in times of cross-strait disagreement, Singapore's neighbours can threaten to cut water supplies. Singapore has now launched plans to process South China Sea water into drinking water – around 30 million gallons every day which will make up around 10% of Singapore's overall water consumption. Ex-ocean water is said to taste 'different' but locals will probably be more open to this plan than a previous scheme to process sewage water.

Displays cater for a range of ages – the enjoyable **Discovery Zone** is aimed at four- to 12-year-olds featuring pieces designed by Paris' Parc de la Villette. Other highlights include the **Web of Life** exhibition, **Eco Garden** and the **Hall of IT** where your youngsters can master the art of video conferencing before they can even reach the first step of the corporate ladder.

Other exhibits suggest corporate sponsorship and education make strange bedfellows, such as a beer-making exhibit sponsored by Singapore Breweries. On another odd note, it's disturbing to see entire families queuing up to take turns on the electric shock chair.

A highlight is the free **Kinetic Garden**, an interactive scientific sculpture garden outside. If the mere thought of running around in the daytime gives you heat stroke it's also open by night. Alternatively you can cool down with a visit to **Snow City** next door (see p. 49).

DON'T MISS
- Thunderbolt! show • Turbo Kourier virtual reality game
- real chickens hatching out of their eggs

SINGAPORE ZOOLOGICAL GARDENS & NIGHT SAFARI   (2, C7)

There's no argument that the Singapore zoo really rocks. Set on 28 hectares of landscaped gardens surrounding a beautiful lake, the zoo is a far cry from the sad concrete enclosures of yesteryear.

INFORMATION

- ✉ 80 Mandai Lake Rd
- ☎ 6269 3411, 24 hr info line 6269 3412
- e www.zoo.com.sg; www.nightsafari.com.sg
- 🚌 138 from Ⓜ Ang Mo Kio
- ⏲ zoo: 8.30am-6pm daily; night safari: 7.30pm-midnight (restaurants open 6.30pm)
- $ zoo: $12/5; night safari: $15.45/10.30 plus tram $5/2; combined zoo & safari package $23/13
- ⓘ information desk; volunteer rangers at the night safari; no feeding the animals or flash photography
- ♿ good
- ✕ on-site restaurants or bring a picnic

Spot a leopard on the trail.

The zoo is home to nearly 3000 animals representing over 150 species of mammals, birds and reptiles. Endangered species include the white rhino, the Komodo dragon, Malayan tiger and a large colony of orang-utan. The zoo boasts a large **primate collection** which offers a great opportunity to see how our cousins live. Just think – if we had evolved slightly differently we humans might've found ourselves behind bars with a bunch of gawking chimpanzees waving video cameras at us.

The zoo itself is constantly evolving and offering new exhibits, the latest being the 'Hamadryas Baboons – The Great Rift Valley of Ethiopia' enclosure. Built over two years at a cost of $2.4 million the exhibit attempts to convey an entire ecosystem: animal, plant, human. Visitors can stand behind a glass window and watch a whole troop of 50 red-bummed baboons at play.

If possible visit at closing time, the start of the **Night Safari**. Clamber aboard the tram for a night drive through the zoo where from the safety of your seat you can smell the stinky rhinos, hear the horrible cries of the golden jackal and see tigers gnawing on huge chunks of steak – all under a well-positioned spotlight. Don't forget to get off and explore the paths.

DON'T MISS
- Breakfast or Going Bananas High Tea with an Orang-utan • Fragile Forest Tour (11.15am unless raining) • award-winning restrooms! • zoo and night safari animal shows • night safari Malayan fruit bats

SRI MARIAMMAN TEMPLE (3, M4)

Paradoxically set in the heart of Chinatown the Sri Mariamman Temple is the oldest Hindu temple in Singapore. It's hard to miss the technicolour *gopuram* (tower) over the entrance gate that identifies this as a temple in the South Indian Dravidian style. Sacred cows are dotted about the boundary wall surrounding the temple while the gopuram is covered in plasterwork images of that Hindu gang of three: Brahma the Creator, Vishnu the Preserver and Shiva the Destroyer. The actual temple is dedicated to the healing goddess Sri Mariamman, a village favourite among Tamils for her rain-bringing powers and reputation for curing disease and sickness – a clue to the tough conditions endured in Singapore during the 1800s.

INFORMATION

- ✉ 244 South Bridge Rd
- ☎ 6223 4064
- Ⓜ Raffles City
- 🚌 124, 174
- ⏰ 7.30am-8.30pm
- 💲 free entry; $3/6 fee for photography/ video cameras
- ⓘ English brochure available at the desk
- ✕ Chinatown (see pp. 75-7)

Naraina Pillai, a trader who arrived in Singapore with Sir Stamford Raffles himself, first built a wooden temple on this site in 1827. The present stone building dates to 1862 although since then it has undergone many renovations, usually in preparation for consecration ceremonies that take place on a 12-year cycle.

Devotees offer initial prayers to the shrine of Sri Vinayagar – the Lord of beginnings and remover of obstacles – before giving prayers and sometimes offerings, such, as fruit and incense, to other deities. It is important to maintain eye contact when receiving blessings, which is why people line up directly in front of the shrines. Only the loincloth-clad priests are allowed to enter the deity's inner sanctum.

Deities in every colour of the rainbow.

Around October each year the temple is the scene for the **Thimithi festival**, during which devotees queue up along South Bridge Rd to walk barefoot over burning coals.

DON'T MISS	• beautiful ceiling frescoes • Thimithi Festival (October)

THIAN HOCK KENG TEMPLE (3, M5)

Also known as the Temple of Heavenly Happiness, this is one of Singapore's oldest and most splendid temples. Dedicated to Ma Zhu Po, goddess of the sea,

INFORMATION

- ✉ 158 Telok Ayer St
- ☎ 6222 8212
- Ⓜ Tanjong Pagar
- ⏲ 8.30am-5.30pm
- $ free
- ✕ Chinatown
  (see pp. 75-7)

it was built on the site of a joss house between 1839 and 1942 by early Hokkien immigrants from China in thanks for safe passage across the sea to Singapore. Before land reclamation shifted it about 500m inland the temple fronted the sea.

Built in the 19th-century Chinese architectural style it remains faithful to the principles of feng shui with open, internal courtyards surrounded by pavilions. No trouble was spared in its construction: the statue of Ma Zhu Po was shipped from China, the decorative tiles were imported from Holland, the cast-iron railings from Scotland. It was built using traditional joinery (no nails!) by skilled builders and artisans – also imported from China.

As you look around the temple, renovated in 2000, you'll see the twin rooftop dragons which represent the principles of yin and yang, two stone lions who guard the door and – as security back-up – fierce-looking portraits of door gods who prevent evil spirits from entering. Overhead the ceilings bear gilded intricate carvings of Chinese folkloric stories and heroes.

Inside you'll find shrines dedicated to the popular goddess of mercy, Guan Yin, and the moon goddess Yue Gong Niang Niang.

Chinese Temples

Many Chinese temples, whether Buddhist, Taoist or Confucian, share similar design elements. There's usually a furnace in front of the temple where prayers, incense and ghost money (symbolic tender for use in the afterlife) are burnt to appease the ancestors. A screen will often separate the entrance from the main hall, where an image of the deity to whom the temple is dedicated is fronted by an altar. Funerary tablets dedicated to deceased members of the community are displayed, often in a separate room. When visiting temples always remember that they are places of worship; remove your shoes and restrict photography to sculptures and architecture.

Exquisite Chinese design at the Thian Hock Keng Temple.

sights & activities

NEIGHBOURHOODS

Most of Singapore's tourist action is centred around the **Orchard Rd**, **Chinatown** and **Little India** areas (see the Highlights chapter), however there are other neighbourhoods worth exploring.

The Marina   (3)

Singapore was founded along the river and recent years have seen widespread attempts to revamp the area with variable results. It's only a matter of time before all the crumbling warehouses are turned into restaurants and yuppie residential areas. Overdevelopment has transformed Boat Quay into a trashy restaurant precinct while Clarke Quay has never really taken off, but the Gallery Hotel and Zouk night-club near Robertson Quay are great nightspots. You can explore the quays by boat tour or water taxi but the river also makes for a lovely moonlit walk.

East Coast   (5)

The **East Coast Park** is a popular recreational haunt for Singaporeans. This is the best spot for swimming, windsurfing, lying around on the sand, renting bikes or inline skates, or eating yourself silly (again!) at a beachfront restaurant. The beach was born of reclaimed land and while it's hardly a tropical paradise, it is a good spot to get away from it all.

> ### Off the Beaten Track
> Simply avoiding Orchard Rd, the main tourist sites and organised tours will quickly get you off the beaten track. Otherwise try a park or Pulau Ubin mid-week, have tea or coffee at one of the hawker stalls in Little India, or take the train to Tiong Bahru for lunch at the markets before a meander around the neighbourhood and a gawk at its quirky 1950s-style apartment buildings.

Going bananas in Little India.

Farther inland are the interesting areas of Geylang and Katong, both largely Malay districts, which are rarely frequented by tourists. **Geylang** is about as close to a 'Little Malaysia' as you'll find, though don't expect thatch-roofed cottages or folk walking about in sarongs – it looks pretty much like everywhere else in Singapore. Most of the activity is focused around **Geylang Serai Market** on Geylang Rd – this place really takes off during Ramadan when the whole area comes alive with night markets. The alleys off Geylang Rd harbour Singapore's most active red-light district.

From the Geylang Serai Market you can head down Joo Chiat Rd to East Coast Rd and explore the old Peranakan neighbourhood of **Katong**, which used to front the coastline until land reclamation moved the beach.

By night the area bustles with seedy karaoke joints, by day the vibe can be pretty sleepy. It's worth looking around the backstreets where you might find old terraces, traditional coffee shops and temples. On Koon Seng Rd, just off Joo Chiat Rd, you'll see some fine **Peranakan terraces** decorated with plaster stucco dragons, birds, crabs and brilliantly glazed tiles.

Changi Village (2, D14)

Changi, on the east coast of Singapore, is an escape from the hubbub of central Singapore but it doesn't offer a lot to do. Singaporeans cross town to eat at the hawker centre in the village and you can camp and swim along the beach – again it's not exactly paradise but the water is wet. You can catch ferries to **Pulau Ubin** (see p. 28) from the village jetty.

Toilet Humour

In a city where non-flushers can be fined and the Ministry of Environment holds an annual Cleanest Toilet Contest it was fitting that Singapore host the first ever World Toilet Summit aimed at promoting the improvement of the toilet environment on an international scale. Organised by the Restroom Association of Singapore, the summit's sponsors included the United Nations Environment Programme and the Singapore Society for Continence. International delegations wrangled over a range of delicate issues from rest room renovation, design, hygiene, ventilation and water conservation. The conference was opened with a riveting mime performance depicting 'desirable and undesirable toilet behaviour'.

Room For Love

Visitors to Geylang will notice strips of dodgy karaoke clubs and numerous budget hotels offering low rates for 'hourly' and 'transit' visitors. While these venues are undoubtedly patronised by sex workers and clients they also attract young couples looking for a bit of privacy. While married couples enjoy government subsidised housing and cash grants, singles may not buy new or re-sale government housing until they are aged 35. Flat sharing with friends is not popular in Singapore, so many young people live with their parents until they are over 30. Given the scarcity of alternatives a budget hotel quickie may well be the best option.

I see nothing…

MUSEUMS

Asian Civilisations Museum (3, H5)
This excellent museum which complements the flagship branch at Empress Place (see p. 16) specialises in displays of Chinese and Peranakan cultures – the latter being the rich intermingling of Chinese, Malay and European ways. Rotating exhibits cover other aspects of Singaporean life from Islam to textiles. There are kids' activities on Sundays.
- ✉ **39 Armenian St**
- ☎ **6332 3015** **e** www .museum.org.sg **Ⓜ City Hall** 🚌 **97, 124, 167**
- ☼ **Tues-Sun 9am-6pm (Fri to 9pm)** Ⓢ **$3/1.50; free Fri 6pm-9pm**
- ♿ **good**

Battle Box (3, G4)
VIPs, defence ministers and military buffs alike climb Fort Canning Hill to visit this excellent museum on the site of Singapore's largest underground military operations complex during WWII. Veterans from around the world and Britain's Imperial War Museum helped recreate the bunker environs. Life-sized models re-enact the fateful decision on 15 Feb 1942 to surrender Singapore to the Japanese.
- ✉ **51 Canning Rise**
- ☎ **6333 0510**
- Ⓜ **Dhoby Ghaut**
- ☼ **Tues-Sun 10am-6pm**
- Ⓢ **$8/5** ♿ **good**

Fuk Tak Chi Museum
(3, M5) Here's a break from all that high-tech interactivity. Standing on the site of Singapore's first temple you can check out relics of olden-day Chinatown, from finely wrought jewellery to opium lamps, while appreciating the traditional architecture.
- ✉ **Telok Ayer St**
- ☎ **6523 7868**
- Ⓜ **Raffles Place**
- ☼ **10am-10pm** Ⓢ **free**

Images of Singapore
(1, B3) You won't find much in the way of artefacts and the speaking mannequins do get on your nerves, but the museum does a great job of explaining how modern Singapore came to be and what life was like during the early times. Typically the pre-Raffles and Communist eras are glossed over. The Festivals of Singapore exhibit is interesting but overly exhaustive.
- ✉ **Cable Car Rd, Sentosa Island** ☎ **6275 0426** 🚌 **Sentosa Service A from Seah Im Bus Terminal (opposite World Trade Centre), E from Orchard Rd, C from Ⓜ Tiong Bahru** 🚠 **from World Trade Centre** 🚢 **from World Trade Centre** ☼ **9am-9pm** Ⓢ **$8/5** ♿ **good**

Singapore History Museum (3, G5)
This grand old museum looks like a poor cousin compared to the whizz-bang new Asian Civilisations Museum. Feature exhibits include: the portrait gallery of bigwigs who have shaped Singapore from Stamford Raffles and Queen Elizabeth to Lee Kuan Yew; the 3D Singapore Story; historical dioramas; and the Secret Societies exhibit complete with cautionary tales by reformed teen gang members about how gang activities and good O level results just don't mix.
- ✉ **93 Stamford Rd**
- ☎ **6332 3251** **e** www .museum.org.sg **Ⓜ City Hall** ☼ **Tues-Sun 9am-6pm (Fri to 9pm)**
- Ⓢ **$3/1.50/8; free Fri 6-9pm**
- ♿ **ground floor only**

Singapore Philatelic Museum (3, H5)
Housed in a 1908 colonial building this museum is more general and dynamic that the subject matter suggests. Exhibits explore what stamps suggest about a country's development and how they contribute to national identity and propaganda campaigns. Kids will enjoy designing stamps and other interactive displays.
- ✉ **23B Coleman St**
- ☎ **6337 3888** **e** www .spm.org.sg **Ⓜ City Hall** ☼ **Tues-Sun 9am-6pm** Ⓢ **$2/1**

URA Gallery (3, N4)
Until the 1950s most Singaporeans were living in simple single-storey homes in *kampongs* (traditional Malay villages). Today 90% of people live in government built high-rise flats. Don't expect much critique but the gallery provides insight into Singapore's conservation plans and how it came to be a planned city. It features an 11m x 11m scale model of the city.
- ✉ **URA Centre, 45 Maxwell Rd** ☎ **6321 8321** Ⓜ **Tanjong Pagar** ☼ **Mon-Fri 9am, 4.30pm, Sat 9am-12.30pm** Ⓢ **free**

GALLERIES

In addition to those listed below you'll find several galleries in the brightly coloured, faux colonial MITA Building (140 Hill St; 3, J5; ⓜ City Hall). Many galleries are closed on Mondays.

Art-2 Gallery (3, J5)
This recommended commercial gallery specialises in contemporary South-East Asian sculpture but also represents regional ceramicists and painters (including Wang Meng Leng, Poh Siew Wah and Desmond Sim).
✉ #01-03 MITA Building, 140 Hill St
☎ 6338 8713 🅴 www.art2.com.sg ⓜ City Hall
🕐 Mon-Sat 11am-7pm
💲 free ♿ good

Bhaskar's Arts Gallery (3, D6)
This non-profit arts group recently landed new digs in Little India's Kerbau Rd, thanks to the National Arts Council housing program. Bhaskar's promotes art by Indian artists from Singapore, India and Malaysia. Works can be a little hit and miss depending on your taste for naive abstract-realist paintings. Also check out **Plastique Kinetic Worms** gallery at No 61.
✉ 19 Kerbau Rd
☎ 6396 4523 🅴 www.bhaskarsartsacademy.com 🚌 65, 97, 106
🕐 Tues-Sun 10am-7pm
💲 free

Christie's International Singapore (4, A5)
Christie's conducts twice yearly auctions of jewellery and art works by Singaporean and regional artists, usually around March/April and September/October.
✉ Unit 3 Parklane,

Goodwood Park Hotel, 22 Scotts Rd ☎ 6235 3828 🅴 www.christies.com ⓜ Orchard
🕐 Mon-Fri 9.30am-6pm
💲 free

Earl Lu Gallery (2, F10) Attached to the LaSalle-SIA College of the Arts, this vibrant gallery specialises in contemporary visual arts and aims to

Street Sculpture

Visitors to Singapore should keep an eye out for public sculpture by acclaimed local and international artists.

- *Abundance* by Sun Yu Li (Suntec City; 3, H8)
- *Between Sea and Sky* by Olivier Strehelle (Marina Mandarin Hotel, 6 Raffles Blvd; 3, J8)
- *Bird* by Fernando Botero (UOB Plaza, by the Fullerton Hotel; 3, K7)
- *Homage to Newton* by Salvador Dali (UOB Plaza, Boat Quay; 3, L6)
- *LOVE* by Robert Indiana (Stamford Rd, near Fort Canning bus stop; 3, G5)
- *Progress and Advancement* by Yang Ying Feng (Raffles Place; 3, L6)
- *Reclining Figures* by Henry Moore (OCBC Building, Chulia St; 3, L5)
- *Six Brushstrokes* by Roy Liechtenstein (Millenia Walk, 9 Raffles Blvd; 3, H9)

Singaporean sculpture: from fabulous Fort Canning…

promote technical and conceptual innovation. It also hosts arts events and talks. The college also has regular exhibits at the more central Gallery Hotel, on Robertson Quay.

✉ **LaSalle-SIA College of the Arts, 90 Goodman Rd** ☎ **6334 4300** e **www.lasallesia.edu.sg** Ⓜ **Aljunied** ◷ **Tues-Fri 11am-7pm, Sat-Sun 10am-5pm** ⓢ **free**

Plastique Kinetic Worms (3, D6)

This is Singapore's only artist-run, non-profit gallery promoting the works of young and contemporary conceptual artists who find it hard to exhibit in more commercial spaces. If you're looking for the avant-garde – this is where you're mostly likely to find it.

✉ **61 Kerbau Rd** ☎ **6292 7783** e **www.pkworms.org.sg** 🚍 **65, 97, 106** ◷ **Tues-Sun noon-7pm** ⓢ **free**

Plum Blossoms (3, H7)

Established in Hong Kong with a branch in New York this upmarket gallery specialises in Asian antiquities (textiles, metalwork and decorative arts) as well as representing contemporary artists from China, Hong Kong, Vietnam and Singapore. The gallery has placed works in national art museums in New York, London and Australia.

✉ **#02-37 Raffles Hotel Arcade** ☎ **6334 1198** e **www.plumblossoms.com** Ⓜ **City Hall** ◷ **Tues-Sun 11am-8pm** ⓢ **free** ♿ **good**

Sculpture Square

(3, F6) Housed in a historic chapel the Sculpture Square is a non-profit gallery exhibiting works by Singaporean artists. It specialises in contemporary sculpture and paintings in a range of styles.

✉ **155 Middle Rd** ☎ **6333 1055** e **www.sculpturesq.com.sg** 🚍 **56, 81, 980** ◷ **Tues-Fri 11am-6pm, Sat-Sun noon-6pm** ⓢ **free**

Soobin Art Gallery

(3, J5) This terrific gallery introduced Singapore to China's vibrant avant-garde scene. It represents contemporary artists working in a range of styles from the photorealism of Ai Xuan, to the pop art of Fang Lijun and Zhu Qizhan's traditional brush painting.

✉ **#01-10/11/12 MITA Building, 140 Hill St** ☎ **6392 9366** e **shop.asiaone.com/stores/soobinart** Ⓜ **City Hall** ◷ **Mon-Sat 11am-7pm, Sun 11am-5pm** ⓢ **free** ♿ **good**

Substation (3, H5)

This non-profit arts centre situated in a disused power station still crackles with creativity. Devoted to nurturing the brave and the new the gallery features a regular turnover of works by young, contemporary artists. The **Guinness Theatre** (p. 101) and **Fat Frog Café** (p. 83) are also on site.

✉ **45 Armenian St** ☎ **6337 7535** e **www.substation.org** Ⓜ **City Hall** 🚍 **97, 124, 167** ⓢ **free**

...to hanging out at the History Museum.

PLACES OF WORSHIP

Armenian Church
(3, H5) Designed by GD Coleman (who also designed St Andrew's, p. 43) and built in 1835, the elegant, neo-classical Armenian Church of St Gregory the Illuminator is Singapore's oldest church. In the graveyard you'll see the tombstone of Agnes Joaquim who 'discovered' the hybrid orchid that later become Singapore's national flower – the Vanda Miss Joaquim.
✉ **60 Hill St** ☎ **6334 0141** Ⓜ **City Hall** Ⓢ **free**

Central Sikh Temple
(3, A8) This striking, modern temple received a Singaporean Architectural Design Award in 1986 and is the main focus for religious and community activities by Singapore's 15,000-strong Sikh community.
✉ **cnr Towner & Serangoon Rds** Ⓜ **Lavender** 🚌 **65, 97, 106** Ⓢ **free**

Fuk Tak Chi (Hock Teck See) Temple
(3, P5) Dwarfed by skyscrapers this little temple, built in 1819, is one of Singapore's oldest. Inside

Temple Etiquette
Remember to remove your shoes when entering temples. Respect those at prayer and be prepared to cover your head at mosques. Entry to mosques is not permitted during prayer time.

incense spirals hang smoking from the ceiling.
✉ **Palmer Rd** Ⓜ **Tanjong Pager** Ⓢ **free**

Kuan Yin Temple
(3, F7) Dedicated to the much-loved goddess of mercy, Guan Yin, this modern temple (1982) is one of Singapore's busiest. Flower sellers and fortune-tellers crowd the entry and worshippers pack into the central pavilion. For extra insurance pragmatic worshippers may also call in to burn incense at the Hindu temple next door.
✉ **Waterloo St** Ⓜ **Bugis** Ⓢ **free**

Leong San See (Dragon Mountain) Temple (3, A8)
Built in 1917 and attached to a boisterous primary school this beautiful Taoist/Buddhist temple has a happy atmosphere. Modelled on a Chinese palace and named for a Tang dynasty temple in China, it was built using traditional joinery and features ceiling beams carved with birds, dragons, flowers and human figures. The smiling Coming Buddha welcomes you at the door – to promote good feng shui you should walk around clockwise.
✉ **371 Race Course Rd** 🚌 **23, 64, 65, 111, 147** 🕐 **6am-6pm** Ⓢ **free**

Monkey God Temple (T'se Tien Tai Seng Yeh) (3, L1)
This is Singapore's best-known monkey temple. A black flag out front means the temple medium is in residence – you may see him at work in the main

shrine around 2pm. The birthday of the monkey god is celebrated in September/October; at this time mediums pierce their cheeks and tongues and go into a state of trance.
✉ **cnr Eng Hoon St & Tiong Poh Rd** Ⓜ **Tiong Bahru** Ⓢ **free**

Ghost Marriage
In Chinese tradition, if a young girl dies before she marries her family may approach a matchmaker to find a family who has similarly lost their son so that the two might marry and be spared from wandering the afterlife alone. At the marriage ceremony the bride, groom and wedding presents are represented by paper effigies that are burnt before the two families share a celebratory feast. Ties between the two families are usually enduring.

St Andrew's Cathedral (3, J6)

Named for the patron saint of Scotland, St Andrew's Cathedral (completed 1861) was built in early English Gothic style using Indian slave labour thoughtfully supplied by the British Empire. It owes its white sheen to a mixture of shell lime, egg white and sugar.

✉ **11 St Andrews Rd**
☎ **6337 6104** Ⓜ **City Hall** 🚌 **7, 124** ⊘ **daily services 7am, 8am, 11am, 2pm, 5pm**
$ **free**

Seng Wong Beo Temple (3, O4)

Few tourists visit this 19th-century temple just minutes from Chinatown's markets. The temple is dedicated to the city god who is responsible for the city's well-being and for leading souls to the underworld. Come Chinese New Year the deities' mouths are smeared with honey to sweeten their words when they report the deeds of mortals to the netherworld. This is the only temple in Singapore to perform ghost marriages.

✉ **cnr Seah & Peck Sts**
Ⓜ **Tanjong Pagar**
$ **free**

Sri Srinivasa Perumal

(3, B8) Dating from 1855 and dedicated to Vishnu (aka Perumal) this is one of Singapore's most important temples and is the kick-off point of the annual Thaipusam procession. Inside the temple you'll see a statue of Vishnu, his consorts Lakshmi and Andal, and his bird-mount, Garuda. The most vibrant time to visit is Sunday evening.

✉ **397 Serangoon Rd**
☎ **6298 5771**
🚌 **23, 64, 111, 147** ⊘ **6.30am-noon, 6-9pm** $ **free**

Sri Veeramakali-amman Temple (Kali the Courageous)

(3, C6) This Shaivite temple is dedicated to Kali, mother of Ganesh and Murugan, consort of Shiva and bloodthirsty warrior against evil. Kali, who is a bit of a babe, has always been popular in Bengal, the birthplace of the labourers who built this temple in 1881. In 2000 craftsmen repainted the figures that line the upper walls, using wildly clashing colours.

✉ **141 Serangoon Rd**
☎ **6294 7175** 🚌 **23, 65, 103, 111** ⊘ **8am-noon, 5.30-8.30pm**
$ **free**

Sultan Mosque (3, E8)

Named for Sultan Hussein Shah – whom Raffles backed as Sultan – this is the largest mosque in Singapore, accommodating 5000 worshippers. Originally built in 1825, it was replaced by this magnificent

A Veiled Affair

In the 1990s France made international headlines when it banned a couple of young Muslim schoolgirls from attending their public, secular school unless they agreed to remove their veils. In 2002 Singapore did the same, suspending three Islamic schoolgirls after they defied a ban on the wearing of the *tudung*, or Islamic headscarf, to class. Following on the heels of 13 arrests in Singapore of suspected terrorists with links to the Al-Qaeda, the incident seems to highlight wider issues about balancing the expression of ethnic identity within Singapore's multi-cultural society with the small state's need for social cohesion.

In Singapore newspapers come in assorted languages.

golden-domed building around 100 years later. Outside prayer time the prayer hall is used for personal meditation – and the

Splendid Sultan Mosque.

odd snooze.

✉ **3 Musca St**
☎ 6293 4405 Ⓜ **Bugis**
🕑 **5am-8.30pm (no entry Fridays)** Ⓢ **free or by donation**

Temple of 1000 Lights (Sakya Muni Buddha Gaya Temple) (3, A8)

Founded in 1927, this rather garish, Thai-style temple is dominated by a 15m, 300-tonne statue of Sakyamuni Buddha in cheery saffron. The temple features an eclectic range of deities from the Chinese Guan Yin to the Hindu Ganesh. Features include the enormous mother-of-pearl replica Buddha footprint complete with 108 auspicious marks. For around 50c you can have your fortune told near the prayer hall.

✉ **366 Race Course Rd**
☎ 6294 0714 🚌 **23, 64, 106, 111, 130, 147**
🕑 **8am-4.45pm**
Ⓢ **free**

PARKS & GARDENS

Also see Bukit Timah (p. 17), Fort Canning (p. 22), Mt Faber (p. 25) and Singapore Botanic Gardens (p. 32).

Bukit Batok Nature Park (2, E6)

This 36-hectare park was developed around a water-filled quarry in 1988. It offers some pleasant walks, lookout points, jogger's trails and a small memorial dedicated to the end of WWII.

✉ **cnr Bukit Batok East Ave 2 & Bukit Batok East Ave 6**
☎ **1800 471 7300, 6292 9560** 🅔 **www .nparks.gov.sg** 🚌 **61, 66, 157, 185, 521, 970**
🕑 **7am-7pm** Ⓢ **free**
♿ **some access**

Chinese & Japanese Gardens (2, E5)

These 13-hectare gardens, featuring a 176-step pagoda and teahouses by Jurong Lake, and supposedly based on the classical style of Beijing's Summer Palace and 14th- to 17th-century Japanese landscape techniques, fall short of their boast. Still, the Zen

Indulge your flower fetish: ogle an orchid.

rock gardens are peaceful and the Chinese garden has a good bonsai collection. On weekends they're overrun with photographers and wedding couples.

✉ **1 Chinese Garden Rd** Ⓜ **Chinese Gardens**
🕑 **9am-6pm** Ⓢ **free**
♿ **good**

East Coast Park

(2, G12) This is a good one for families: hire bikes or inline skates and zoom off up and down the paths, enjoy a shady walk, take a dip in the sea or chill out with a beer at a beachfront restaurant.

✉ **East Coast Parkway** 🚌 **16** ⑤ **free** ♿ **good**

Mandai Orchid Gardens (2, C7)

Explore four solid acres of Singapore's most famous flower displayed over a hilly garden setting not far from the zoo. The park also offers international delivery of orchid gift-boxes.

✉ **Mandai Lake Rd** ☎ **6269 1036** 🚌 **138 from ⓂAng Mo Kio** or 🚌 **927 from ⓂChoa Chu Kang** ⏰ **8.30am-5.30pm** ⑤ **$2/0.50**

MacRitchie Reservoir

(2, E8) Surrounded by jungle this 12-hectare park and the nearby **Upper Peirce** and **Upper Seletar** reservoirs offer a pleasant city retreat. Here you'll find jogging tracks, an exercise area, kids playground and tea kiosk. A band often plays on Sunday (check the newspapers).

✉ **Lornie Rd** 🚌 **157 from ⓂToa Payoh** ⑤ **free**

National Orchid Garden (2, F8)

Set in Singapore's Botanic Gardens this garden offers one of the world's most extensive orchid displays – around 700 species and 2000 hybrids – in a pleasant setting.

✉ **Singapore Botanic Gardens, Cluny Rd** ☎ **6471 9955** 🚌 **7, 77, 105, 106, 123, 174** ⏰ **8.30am-7pm** ⑤ **$2/1.50** ♿ **good**

Pasir Ris Park (2, D13)

Even on weekends this park is surprisingly quiet. Bring the kids and hire bikes (training-wheel models available) for some old-fashioned quality time. Finish off with a round of ice creams and a family sing-along.

✉ **Pasir Ris Rd** 🚌 **354 from ⓂPasir Ris** ⏰ **7am-7pm** ⑤ **free** ♿ **good**

Sungei Buloh Nature Park (2, B4)

Bird lovers should pack their binoculars – this 87-hectare wetland nature reserve is home to 140 species of birds, most of which are migratory. The park features mangrove boardwalks, walking trails, a visitors centre, bird observation huts and guided tours (Saturday only, 9am, 10pm, 3pm, 4pm). The best time for bird spotting is early morning.

✉ **301 Neo Tiew Cres** ☎ **6794 1401** 🄴 **www .sbnp.org** 🚌 **925 from ⓂKranji: Mon-Sat alight at Kranji Reservoir car park for a 15min walk to the park; Sun & public hols bus stops at park entrance** ⏰ **Mon-Sat 7.30am-7pm, Sun 7am-7pm** ⑤ **$1/0.50** ♿ **good**

Lush green lawns at the Singapore Botanic Gardens are perfect for a picnic.

QUIRKY SINGAPORE

Astrology (3, D6)
Astrology shops are clustered around the Little India Arcade and Campbell St where you can have your fortune told, your chart drawn up or learn if you share a destiny with your chosen one.
✉ **Little India** 🚌 **65, 97, 106** ⑤ **varies**

Bird Singing (3, K1)
Get up early and greet the bird enthusiasts who gather daily to drink coffee and hear their birds sing. Each bird is housed in a delicately decorated lacquered bamboo cage suspended from numbered hooks near the local coffee shop, which keeps everyone plied with *kopi* and *kaya* toast (coffee and coconut toast).
✉ **cnr Tiong Bahru & Seng Poh Rds** Ⓜ **Tiong Bahru** ⊙ **7am-11am, Sundays are best** ⑤ **free**

Festival of the Hungry Ghosts (3, L4)
Every August or September the gates of hell are opened for a month and the hungry ghosts return to earth to haunt their relatives who must appease them. This is a time for huge banquets, street opera, puppet shows and burning of miniature paper effigies of 'hell money', mobile phones, cars and anything else you might need to keep up with the Joneses in the afterlife.
✉ **Chinatown or housing estates** ⑤ **free**

Fountain of Wealth
(3, H8) It boasts a water jet of 30m and weighs 85 tonnes, yet the world's largest fountain is not necessarily the world's most tasteful one. By night (8-10pm) a laser and sound show offers you an unrivalled opportunity to project an 18m personalised message onto the water curtain – what better way is there to say 'I love you'?
✉ **5 Temasek Blvd** ☎ **6295 2888** ℮ **www.sunteccity.com.sg/wealth** Ⓜ **City Hall** 🚌 **36, 133, 501** ⊙ **9am-10pm** ⑤ **free** ♿ **good**

Haw Par Villa Tiger Balm Gardens (2, G7)
This uniquely Singaporean attraction was founded by the heirs to the fortune made from the miracle cure-all Tiger Balm. Featuring around 1000 statues based on Chinese folklore and heroes, it's unbelievably kitsch. The Ten Courts of Hell is the highlight: intriguingly grotesque statues depict sinners'

Haw Par Villas: To teach me a lesson I wouldn't forget, my parents brought me to hell...

'Hell was located in a Dragon's head, and my parents dragged me past the jagged teeth into the belly of the beast...what struck me most about this educational excursion to Hell was that Chinese values were different from mine. In Hell, prostitutes were drowned in a sea of blood, food wasters who didn't finish their meals were sawn in half, and marijuana addicts were tied to a fiery pillar, where they were BBQed. Rapists, robbers and murderers simply had their hands cut off. It seemed odd, and unfair, that some Son of Sam/Fred West sicko would have a less painful time in hell than a pot-smoking hippy who had never finished eating his tofu.'

Mammon Inc, by Hwee Hwee Tan (Michael Joseph 2001).

Ha ha ha! Welcome to hell...

Speak Freely but not Frankly

The establishment of Speakers' Corner in Hong Lim Park (3, K4; near the corner of New Bridge Rd & Upper Pickering St) in 2000 was seen as evidence of Singaporean democracy and a victory for freedom of speech. Hundreds of people turned up to the inauguration, huddling close to hear speakers who, denied microphones, struggled to be heard. During the first month 400 people came to voice their thoughts, but a year later only 11 braved the imposed restrictions. All are free to speak their minds, providing they register their names, steer away from controversial issues, accept all questions from the audience and don't violate Singapore's notorious sedition laws... And non-Singaporeans can forget giving out some friendly advice to the locals, as they are banned.

fates in lurid detail.
✉ 262 Pasir Panjang Rd ☎ 6774 0300
🚌 200 from Ⓜ Buona Vista ⏲ 9am-6pm
⑤ $5/2.50

Mustafa Centre & Desker Rd (3, C7)

Sunday evening sees around 10,000 Indian men hanging around little India – most of the action takes place around the Mustafa Centre electronics shopping complex and the car park across Serangoon Rd. Not far from here on Desker Rd ladies of the night and sweet transvestites ply their wares – in a most un-Singaporean fashion, lah!
✉ Serangoon Rd
🚌 65, 97, 106 ⏲ Sun eve ⑤ free

Opera Karaoke

(3, M4) If you fancy yourself as a bit of a Chinese opera star – and who doesn't? – make your way to the Chinese Theatre Circle between 2 and 5pm. Here you can perform all your favourite opera hits – or enjoy the offerings of

other amateurs. Taking the piss is not allowed.
✉ 5 Smith St ☎ 6323 4862 ℮ www.ctcopera .com.sg Ⓜ Outram Park ⏲ 2-5pm ⑤ $10

Sky Dining (2, H8)

Here's an innovation that leaves the revolving restaurant for dead. Impress the pants off the object of your affection with a three-course romantic dinner and sweeping views to Mt Faber and Sentosa Island while swinging 70m above Singapore in a glass-bottomed cable car. It's an interesting spot to get steamy – but a bad spot to break up. Book by 1pm on dining day.
✉ Singapore Cable Car, 109 Mt Faber Rd
☎ 6277 9640
℮ www.cablecar.com .sg 🚌 61, 97, 124, 143, 166 ⏲ Sat 6.30-8.30pm ⑤ $120 per couple ♿ wheelchairs won't fit in cable cars but can be left behind

Quirky TV

Issues of press freedom aside, Singaporean TV lends intriguing insight into the nation's cultural and ethnic demographics. Channel surf between B-grade Hollywood boys and guns flicks, local variety shows, slapstick Cantonese soap operas complete with historical costumes and kung fu and around 40 years' worth of Bollywood musicals. Regardless of genre sex is a no-no but violence is OK!

No sex, please! Talk to the hand.

SINGAPORE FOR CHILDREN

With its safe, clean streets and family-orientated culture, Singapore is a great place for kids. See also Sentosa Island (p. 30), Singapore Zoological Gardens (p. 34), Singapore Science Centre (p. 33) and Jurong Bird Park (p. 23).

Holidays and ice cream go together, just ask them!

at-sunrice (3, G5)

The brochure promises they'll 'learn basic maths skills through baking', but the kids will be too busy baking brownies, dumplings and pizza and playing games to notice there's any maths involved. Activities are suitable for ages 8-10.

✉ **Fort Canning Centre, Cox Terrace** ☎ 6336 3307 **e** www.at-sunrice.com **Ⓜ** Dhoby Ghaut ⏱ Sat 3-5pm **⑤** $30 **&** good

Big Splash (2, G11)

This water fun park is looking a little run-down but that probably won't worry the kids. There's a big slippery waterslide plus swimming pools. Sadly the complex is shadeless (bring sunscreen) and the 'lifeguards' don't seem particularly alert.

✉ **902 East Coast Parkway** ☎ 6345 6762 🚌 16 (to Marine Tce, cross via the underpass) ⏱ Mon-Fri noon-6pm, Sat-Sun 10am-7pm **⑤** $3/2 **&** good (pool only)

Heeren (4, C7)

The Heeren is a good spot for teens to spend their parents' money. There are three floors of CDs at HMV, while levels 4 and 5 boast teen-ware, quirky trinkets, a cafe and pinball parlour.

✉ **260 Orchard Rd** **Ⓜ** Somerset ⏱ 10am-10pm **⑤** free **&** yes

Jurong Reptile Park (2, F4)

It's a little run-down and probably not much fun for the crocs (especially given that they appear on the park restaurant's menu) but kids get a thrill from the croc wrestling, giant tortoises, Komodo dragons and pythons on display.

✉ **241 Jalan Ahmad Ibrahim** ☎ 6261 8866 🚌 194 or 251 from **Ⓜ** Boon Lay ⏱ 9am-6pm; croc show: 11.45am, 2pm; feeding: 10.30am, 5pm **⑤** $7/3.50 **&** good

National Youth Centre Skate Park and Youth Park (4, D7)

If the kids have skates with them this is a great spot to kill a few hours. The Youth Park occasionally hosts live outdoor bands and BMX and skating displays. Behind the centre on Somerset Alley there's a hawker stall selling the best banana fritters in town.

✉ **Somerset Rd** ☎ 6734 4233 **e** www.nyc.youth.gov.sg **Ⓜ** Somerset **⑤** free **&** good

Pretty in Tokyo (3, F7)

Kids go mad for these photo booths. A few dollars will buy you a sheet of sticker photos of yourself and your friends – choose your own background, from *Cosmo* cover girl, ski fields, syrupy love hearts or 'Shark Attack!'

✉ **#03-08 Parco Bugis Junction** ☎ 6334 7707 **Ⓜ** Bugis ⏱ 11am-9pm **⑤** a few dollars

---

Babysitting

The **YMCA Metropolitan** (60 Stevens Rd; 4, A4; ☎ 6731 0763; **e** www.mymca.org.sg) operates a creche open to anyone with children on weekdays from 9am to noon at a charge of $15 per day. For all other times the best option is to ask your hotel to organise babysitting for you. Usually they will allocate their own staff to the task.

Skating up a storm.

Snow City (2, F5)

If they're getting a little tired of the tropical weather, here kids can throw snowballs and toboggan down the slopes on snowtubes to their hearts' content. Actually, it's quite fun for grown-ups too. Entrance price includes snow jackets and snow boots – bring socks.
✉ **21 Jurong Town Hall Rd** ☎ **6560 0179**
e www.snowcity.com.sg 🚌 66, 178, 182 from Ⓜ **Jurong East**
🕐 Tues-Sun 9am-8.30pm ⑤ peak (Sat-Sun & hols) $12/12/39, off-peak $8/8/25; glove hire $1.50

Underwater World

(1, B2) Start off by plunging your arm into the Touch Pool and feeling the slimy de-barbed stingrays, starfish and rough little blind sharks. Check out the sea horses, the elegant jellyfish and vibrantly coloured coral reef before stepping into the Ocean Colony where giant stingrays, nurse sharks and fish swim all around. Entry includes admission to the dolphin show at Dolphin Lagoon (1, D5) at Central Beach.
✉ **80 Siloso Rd, Sentosa Island** ☎ **6275 0030**
e www.underwaterworld.com.sg
🚌 Sentosa Service A from Seah Im Bus Terminal (opposite World Trade Centre), E from Orchard Rd, C from Ⓜ Tiong Bahru 🚡 from World Trade Centre
🚠 from World Trade Centre 🕐 9am-9pm; Dolphin Lagoon: 10.30am-6pm (show times 11am, 1.30pm, 3.30pm, 5.30pm)
⑤ $17/11 (under 12 yrs) or free (under 90cm) ♿ good

Wet Markets

The wet markets at the Chinatown Complex (3, M4; p. 75), Tekka Centre in Little India (3, D6; p. 75) and Geylang Serai Market in Geylang (5, A3; p. 37) are fun in a squelchy, squishy, sticky, gross kind of way. See baskets of stinky dried fish, giant stingrays, slippery eels and black preserved century eggs – so much more exciting than the supermarket.
⑤ free

I'd like to be under the sea… Ride the travellator at Underwater World.

KEEPING FIT

Cycling & Skating

For about $5 you can hire skates and bicycles – including training-wheel and cool low-rider tandem models – from East Coast Park (p. 37), Pasir Ris Park (p. 45), Sentosa Island (p. 30) and Pulau Ubin (p. 28).

California Fitness Centre, Orchard Club
(4, B7) This huge gym features three floors of glass windows and mirrors, perfect for posing, perving – oh, and getting fit. Famous for its aerobic classes, it also offers step, salsa, yoga and hip hop classes.
✉ 1 Grange Rd
☎ 6834 2100
e www.calfitness
.com.hk Ⓜ Somerset
🕓 Mon-Sat 6am-midnight, Sun 8am-10pm ⑤ $30 day pass

Clark Hatch Life Spa
(3, J8) This small, intimate, low-key gym is great for busy business visitors. There are other branches at the Sheraton Towers (p. 105), Orchard Hotel (p. 107) and Inter-Continental Hotel (p. 104).
✉ #04 Pan Pacific Hotel, 7 Raffles Blvd
☎ 6334 5139

Spa Treatment

No matter where you are you can always give those muscles a much-needed limber (we know you're worth it). Consult p. 73 for full contact details for the following spa and/or massage locations.

- Chinatown: **Aspapra** (3, O4; ☎ 6879 2688)
- Colonial area: **Amrita Spa** (3, H7; ☎ 6336 4477)
- Holland Village: **Spa in the Village** (2, F7; ☎ 6467 7219)
- Little India: **Traditional Body Charm** (massage only; 3, D6; ☎ 6336 9411)
- River Valley Rd: **Shiatsu School** (3, H3; ☎ 6836 1231)

Ⓜ Raffles Place
🚌 75, 77, 171, 960
🕓 6.30am-10pm
⑤ $21

Farrer Park Swimming Complex
(3, B5) Most good hotels have swimming pools, but if yours doesn't or it's cramping your style this complex is quite central. Otherwise try the River Valley Swimming Complex (1 River Valley Rd; 3, J4; ☎ 6337 6275).
✉ 2 Rutland Rd
☎ 6299 1002
🕓 8am-9pm ⑤ $2

Hash House Harriers
This international social organisation has a number of mixed and single-sex jogging groups and bike hash groups operating in Singapore. Details of upcoming runs (including meeting points and after-run dinner and drinks) are posted on the website of the Lion City chapter. It has regular Friday runs.
✉ various meeting points ☎ 6345 7431 (Fri only)

Show off your freestyle at Farrer Park…

Start the fitness cycle.

e home.pacific.net.sg/~ken/lchhh.html ⑤ from approx $20 – prices include dinner & drinks

Shambhala Yoga Centre (4, C3)
This slick yoga centre caters to all those human-pretzel needs.
✉ #06-05 Forum Galleria, 583 Orchard Rd

Golf
Singapore has plenty of golf courses, though some are members only or don't allow visitors to play on weekends. A game of golf costs from around $90 on weekdays, and $100 to $220 on weekends. The following courses have 18 holes:

- **Jurong Country Club**
  (9 Science Centre Rd; 2, F5; ☎ 6560 5655)
- **Laguna National Golf & Country Club**
  (11 Laguna Golf Green; 2, F13; ☎ 6541 0289)
- **Raffles Golf Club**
  (450 Jalan Ahmad Ibrahim; 2, F2; ☎ 6861 7655)
- **Sentosa Golf Club**
  (Sentosa Island; 1, D5; ☎ 6275 0022)

☎ 6735 2163 Ⓜ Orchard ⊙ Mon-Fri 9am-9pm, Sat-Sun 10am-5pm ⑤ $28 for a 1.5hr lesson

Singapore Badminton Hall
(2, F10) Like most of South-East Asia, Singapore is mad about badminton. Bookings are essential at these courts on the East Coast.
✉ **102 Guillemard Rd** ☎ 6345 7554 Ⓜ Paya Lebar 🚌 7, 70 ⊙ 8am-11pm ⑤ $7.40 peak, $3.50 off-peak

Singapore Tennis Centre (2, G11)
Just by the East Coast Park, the tennis centre offers courts, racket hire ($5) and lessons ($60 per hr). You should book ahead for peak times and weekends. Bring balls or buy them from the centre.
✉ **1020 East Coast Parkway** ☎ 6449 9034 🚌 16 ⊙ 7am-11pm ⑤ per hr: Mon-Fri $10.50 (7am-6pm), $14.50 (6-11pm); Sat-Sun $14.50

…or grapple with a golf ball.

BUILDINGS & MONUMENTS

Chijmes (3, H6)
This lovely building, formerly known as the Convent of
the Holy Infant Jesus
School, was founded in
1854 and was an orphan-
age and school until 1983.
These days it's a restaurant
and shopping complex. The
fountain, cobbled walkways
and peaceful environment
make for pleasant dining.
✉ **30 Victoria St**
☎ **6332 6279** Ⓜ **City
Hall** ◷ **11am-10pm**
⑤ **free** ♿ **good**

**Civilian War
Memorial** (3, H7)
Also known as the
'Chopsticks', the four soaring pillars of this memorial
represent the Chinese,
Eurasian, Indian and Malay
civilians who were casual-
ties of the Japanese inva-
sion during WWII.
✉ **btw Raffles City &
Marina Sq** Ⓜ **City Hall**
⑤ **free**

Istana (3, D3)
Set well back from the main
road, the neo-Palladian
Istana (palace), home to
Singapore's president, is
only open to the public on
selected holidays (eg, New
Year's). The building was
designed in the 1860s as
Government House and
built at great expense
chiefly to impress the visiting Duke of Edinburgh.
✉ **Orchard Rd**
Ⓜ **Dhoby Ghaut**
◷ **selected public hols
only** ⑤ **free, but passport required**

Kranji War Memorial
(2, C6) The Kranji War
Memorial contains thou-
sands of graves of Allied

troops killed during WWII.
The walls are inscribed
with the names of 24,346
men and women who lost
their lives fighting in
South-East Asia – registers
are also available for
inspection.
✉ **9 Woodlands Rd**
Ⓜ **Kranji** ⑤ **free**

Merlion (3, K7)
This much-photographed
statue (built in 1972) of a
half-lion half-fish symbol-
ises Singaporean tourism,
yet fails to live up to expec-
tations due to its insignifi-
cant stature. Pre-empting
the critics the Singaporeans
built a new, 37m version
with a laser-light show on
Sentosa Island.
✉ **Singapore River
(near Canvenagh
Bridge & the Fullerton
Hotel)** Ⓜ **Raffles Place**
◷ **7am-10pm** ⑤ **free**

Raffles Landing Site
(3, K6) A modern version
of an original bronze statue
(now at Victoria Concert
Hall) stands where Raffles
himself first stepped onto
Singaporean land. He looks
reasonably pleased with
himself.
✉ **Empress Place,
North Boat Quay**
Ⓜ **Raffles Place**
⑤ **free** ♿ **good**

**Sun Yat Sen
Nanyang Memorial
Hall** (2, F9)
This old villa (built in the
1880s) was the one-time
residence of the Chinese rev-
olutionary Republican leader
Sun Yat Sen. The house, a
national monument, is a fine
example of a colonial
Victorian villa and houses
displays of Sun Yat Sen's life
and work.
✉ **12 Tai Gin Rd**
☎ **6256 7377** ℮ **www
.wanqingyuan.com.sg**
🚌 **139, 145 from**
Ⓜ **Toa Payoh** ◷ **Tues-
Sun 9am-5pm** ⑤ **$2**

Total Defence

All Singaporean men between the ages of 18 and 40
must perform annual military service. But this is just
part of Singapore's overall Total Defence program
which aims to promote internal cohesion and presumably some defence against potential invading forces –
Singaporeans have not forgotten the Japanese inva-
sion of WWII. Total Defence encourages individuals to
practise economic, psychological and social defence
and consider acquiring useful skills, such as first aid, or
taking part in voluntary food rationing. Singaporeans
are occasionally subjected to water and electricity rationing in the name of nation building.

out & about

WALKING TOURS
A Passage to India

Take a bus to the corner of Serangoon and Balestier Rds and walk up Balestier for 100m before turning left into Race Course Rd. Heading southwest you'll see crumbling shophouses and the Chinese Leong San See Temple ❶ on your right; almost directly opposite there's the Thai-inspired Temple of 1000 Lights ❷. Further along is the back entrance to the Sri Srinivasa Perumal Temple ❸ – if it's closed cross through Perumal Rd to the entrance on Serangoon Rd. Return to Serangoon and continue southwest, detour to the left for the Mustafa Centre electronics shopping complex ❹, or a peek into the red light district of Desker Rd ❺, before coming to the Sri Veeramakaliamman Temple ❻. Continue down Serangoon and cross over to Kerbau Rd (on the right), passing traditional sari and beauty shops to the restored Peranakan-style building known as Tan House ❼. Cut through the lane near Andhra Curry (see p. 84) to Buffalo Rd and stop at the religious stores or the galleries at No 61 and 19 before exploring the Tekka Centre wet market ❽. Finish up at the Little India Arcade ❾ opposite for an Indian or Sri Lankan meal and a glass of ginger tea. Once refreshed explore the centre for souvenirs or stroll around Clive St and Campbell Lane ❿.

distance 1.5km **duration** 2hrs
- ▶ **start** 🚌 65, 97, 103, 106, 139
- ● **end** Ⓜ Bugis or 🚌 23, 65, 97, 103, 106, 111, 139 (from Jalan Besar)

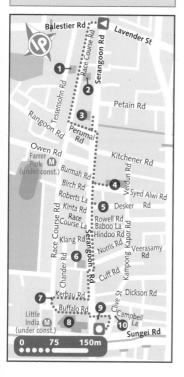

SIGHTS & HIGHLIGHTS

Leong San See Temple (p. 42)
Temple of 1000 Lights (p. 44)
Sri Srinivasa Perumal Temple (p. 43)
Mustafa Centre (p. 46)
Desker Rd (p. 46)
Sri Veeramakaliamman Temple (p. 43)
Andhra Curry (p. 84)
Plastique Kinetic Worms Gallery (p. 41)
Bhaskar's Arts Gallery (p. 40)
Tekka Centre wet market (p. 24)
Little India Arcade (p. 24)

Arabic Amble

From Bugis MRT walk northeast up Victoria St, turn right into Arab St ❶, full of traditional textiles and souvenir shops, and cross North Bridge Rd where you'll see a mosque directly opposite and the Indian Zam Zam restaurant to your left. Continue along Arab St, or take a detour down the

SIGHTS & HIGHLIGHTS

Arab St (pp. 84-5)
Zam Zam (p. 85)
Sultan Mosque (pp. 43-4)

Fit for a Sultan.

small Haji Lane ❷, stopping at the traditional perfumery at No 51, before returning to Arab St. Turn onto Baghdad St before a quick left onto Bussorah St, lined with palm trees and revamped shophouses in pastel shades. Stop at the end to visit the golden-topped Sultan Mosque ❸. Exiting the mosque turn left then a quick right for tasty treats on Kandahar St. Cut through the grassy patch to see the crumbling Istana Kampong Glam ❹, historic seat of the Malay royalty since the 1840s until it was closed in 2000. Return to Kandahar St and proceed north-west back to Victoria St. Cross the road and see the old royal cemetery ❺ with its scattered tombstones and continue northeast to the pretty blue-tiled Malabar Muslim Jama-Ath Mosque ❻. From here you can call it a day or walk southeast along Jalan Sultan and left onto Beach Rd to the Hajjah Fatimah Mosque ❼.

distance 2.5-3km **duration** 2-3hrs
▶ **start** Ⓜ Bugis
● **end** 🚌 7, 63, 103, 124 (from North Bridge Rd) or Ⓜ Bugis, Lavender

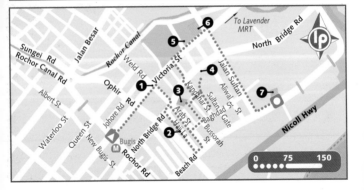

Chinatown Crawl

From Raffles Place MRT walk east along Chulia St and turn left into Phillip St, where on your right-hand side you'll see Wak Hai Cheng Bio Temple ❶. Crossing Church St the road becomes Telok Ayer St, where you'll find Fuk Tak Chi Museum ❷. Just over Boon Tat St is the Nagore Durgha Shrine, an old mosque built by Chulia Muslims from South India ❸, followed by Thian Hock Keng Temple ❹ and the Al-Abrar Mosque ❺. Turn right onto Amoy St, past the hawker centre to Siang Cho Keong Temple ❻. Walk north up Amoy St, turning left onto Cross St and left again down the winding Club St, where you can stop for a beer or a snack. At the bottom is South Bridge Rd; turn right and stop by Eu Yan Sang medical hall ❼ before crossing over and walking north to the Sri Mariamman Temple ❽ and the Jamae Mosque ❾ almost next door. Exit the mosque and turn right into Pagoda St. Explore souvenir stores and traditional Chinese businesses around Pagoda, Trengganu and Sago Sts before finishing up with a hawker-stall meal on Smith St ❿.

SIGHTS & HIGHLIGHTS

Fuk Tak Chi Museum (p. 39)
Thian Hock Keng Temple (p. 36)
Eu Yan Sang medical hall (p. 73)
Sri Mariamman Temple (p. 35)

Intricate design: Thian Hock Keng Temple.

You can also do this walk in reverse, starting in Chinatown and at the end continuing past Raffles Place to Boat Quay ⓫ for a riverside meal and a beer.

distance 2km **duration** 2hrs
▶ **start** Ⓜ Raffles Place
● **end** 🚌 33, 62, 103, 147, 174 (South Bridge Rd) or 2, 33, 81, 124 (North Bridge Rd)

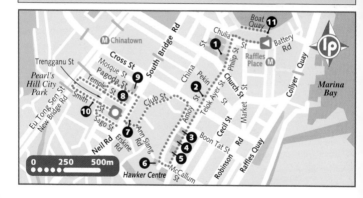

Colonial Loop

Start at Raffles Place MRT and cut through the Clifford Centre to the historic Clifford Pier ❶, walk north up the promenade and admire the Fullerton Hotel ❷ and the Merlion Park ❸. Cross over Anderson Bridge and note the Dalhousie Obelisk ❹, dedicated to free trade, to your left. Turn right up Connaught Dve the Lim Bo Seng Memorial ❺, built in honour of a WWII hero, followed by the Indian National Army Monument ❻. Continue to the British war memorial, the Cenotaph ❼, catching glimpses of the strange-looking Esplanade development behind, and on to the Victorian-style Tan Kim Seng Fountain. Cross Stamford Rd to the Civilian War Memorial ❽.

Then cross back and head down St Andrew's Rd, stopping by St Andrew's Cathedral ❾ just off Coleman St if you wish. Walk south

Cop an eyeful of the fabulous Fullerton.

distance approx 2.5km
duration 2½hrs
► **start** Ⓜ Raffles Place
● **end** Ⓜ Raffles Place or taxi

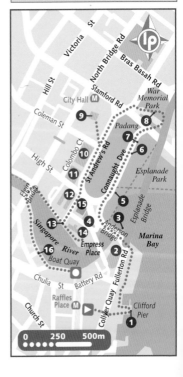

past the imposing City Hall ❿ fronted by the Padang, past the Supreme Court ⓫ to Old Parliament House ⓬. Cut through Old Parliament Lane to Raffles' Landing Site ⓭ before stopping for lunch at Empress Place. Once refreshed you can explore the new Asian Civilisations Museum ⓮, the Victoria Theatre & Concert Hall ⓯ behind it or cross over to Boat Quay ⓰.

EXCURSIONS
Johor Bahru, Malaysia   (2, A6)

Capital of the Malaysian state of Johor, which comprises the entire southern tip of the peninsula, Johor Bahru is the southern gateway to Peninsular Malaysia. Connected to Singapore by the 1.38km-long Causeway, Johor Bahru (or JB as it's usually known) inevitably suffers as a poor relation to its more glamorous neighbour, yet its lively chaos is an interesting contrast to Singapore's squeaky-clean sterility. It is both a breath of fresh air and a bad aroma.

On weekends and public holidays, Singaporeans flock across the Causeway for vice, shopping and excitement, and at these times Johor Bahru puts on a show. Exotic street entertainment is provided by medicinal vendors dangling snakes and promising penis enlargement with their elixirs, and by turbaned *bomohs* (spiritual healers) selling magical 'love oil'. The *kedai gunting rambut* (barber shops) do a great trade too, but in girls not haircuts.

Aside from the seedy exotica, Johor Bahru has the finest **museum** in Malaysia and a thriving **night market**. In the business centre of town are plenty of pavement hawkers and other colourful stalls that are so much a part of Asia but lacking in Singapore.

Be alert, however: Johor Bahru has had some bad press recently, particularly with regard to the personal security of visitors. Keep your wits about you and your belongings close by and you should be OK.

> **INFORMATION**
>
> *30-45mins north of the city*
> 🚌 departs every 15mins btw 6.30am and 11pm from Queen St bus terminal
> ☎ Singapore-Johor Express 6292 8149
> $ bus ticket $2.40
> ✕ *pasar malam* (night market) on Jalan Wong Ah Fook or shopping-mall food courts

St John's & Kusu Islands   (2, J9)

St John's and Kusu Islands both make a pleasant escape from urban Singapore, especially during the week when it's quiet. Both boast safe **swimming lagoons** – although the water can be a little polluted – and shady picnic areas as well as handy changing rooms and toilets. Culinary offerings are limited so pack yourself a picnic. You can explore Kusu in around an hour; check out the turtle sanctuary, the Tua Pek Kong Chinese temple (near the jetty) and Singapore's most popular Malay shrine, **Keramat Kusu**. Hill-top Keramat is popular with couples praying for children – the prayers are marked by pieces of cloth tied around trees on the way up the stairs to the shrine. Around October or November each year Kusu is the site of an important Taoist pilgrimage.

> **INFORMATION**
>
> *6km south of the city*
> ⚓ Singapore Cruise Centre at the World Trade Centre; 30mins to Kusu, 45mins to St John's
> $ ferry tickets $9/6 return

Pulau Bintan   (2, F14)

Indonesia is a mere ferry ride away and the island of Bintan makes a good break from Singapore's urban density. Thus far the island has avoided rampant development, although it's hard to say how long it will maintain its low profile. For the visitor, the main attractions are the relaxed, white-sand beaches of the east coast, luxury beach resorts and the old world charm of Tanjung Pinang (a visa-free entry/exit point), and nearby Pulau Penyenget. Various tour operators offer day-trips to Tanjung Pinang for around $140, but ferry connections don't leave much time for exploring the city, so ideally stay overnight.

Tanjung Pinang is the largest town in the Riau Archipelago but it retains much of its historical feel, particularly the picturesque, stilted section of town that juts over the sea around Jalan Plantar II. Across the harbour is the island of **Pulau Penyenget**, once capital of the kingdom and now harbouring ruins of the old Raja Ali palace and an ornate mosque complete with multiple domes and minarets.

Also across the harbour is the small village of **Senggarang**. Don't miss its star attraction – an old Chinese temple held together by the roots of a huge banyan tree. You can charter a sampan from

INFORMATION

1½hrs (by Dino Shipping or Penguin Ferry Services) or 45min to Bintan Resort (by Bintan Resort Ferries)

🚢 Tanah Merah ferry terminal, or Bintan Resort Ferries

☎ Bintan Resort Ferries 6542 4369, Dino Shipping 6276 9722, Penguin Ferry Services 6271 4866

💲 ferry tickets $38-44/32-36 (return)

Kick back and enjoy island delights.

Tanjung Pinang along the **Sungei Ular** (Snake River) through the mangroves to the Chinese temple, with its gory murals of the trials and tortures of hell.

The best beaches are along the east coast, where there is also good **snorkelling** outside the monsoon season. You'll find the best choice of accommodation at the main beach, Pantai Trikora.

Sisters' & Lazarus Islands

Sisters' (2, K8) and Lazarus Islands (2, J9) are relatively unspoiled and great for swimming, snorkelling and diving in the nearby coral reefs. To get there hire a water taxi from Clifford Pier at Marina Bay. Expect to pay around $50 per hour – the boats can carry from six to 12 people. Bring a picnic, plenty of drinking water and diving and snorkelling gear. Be wary of strong currents when swimming.

Tioman Island   (2, F14)

Tropical Tioman Island is too far away for a day trip but it makes for an ideal long-weekend escape. The largest and most spectacular of Malaysia's east-coast islands, Tioman boasts beautiful beaches, clear water and coral for snorkelling or diving enthusiasts. Favourite pastimes here are splashing on the beach, reading crappy paperbacks and gobbling banana pancakes. The island also offers surprisingly high mountains while lush jungle is just a short walk away from the coast.

INFORMATION

4hrs

🚢 Tanah Merah Ferry Terminal

☎ Tioman Island Resort Ferries 6542 7105

⑤ ferry tickets $148-168/93 ($18 infant) return

Note that Tioman is one of Malaysia's most popular destinations and it can get quite crowded at peak times, particularly in July and August. Accommodation tends to be of the backpacker beach huts and longhouse rooms variety. However more upmarket accommodation can be found at Melina Beach Resort (☎ 013 432 9066) and the international-class Berjaya Tioman Beach Resort (☎ 09 419 1000).

You talkin' to me?

In 1989 the Singaporean government attempted the impossible – it banned taxi drivers from discussing politics and controversial subjects with their passengers. The news mustn't have reached one of our recent drivers who, while cursing the traffic on Orchard Rd, cheerfully proposed blowing up the entire strip and replacing it with one mega-mall – that would hopefully offer massage FOC (free of charge) on the top floor. As in the rest of the world, Singaporean taxi drivers offer the most diverse, if not accurate, range of local opinions. More confusingly, taxi drivers will often insist on asking you to choose between equally bamboozling routes to your destination – it helps if you know the area or nearest main road.

ORGANISED TOURS

If you're pressed for time or simply can't be bothered with the burdensome details of getting around by yourself, tours offer a good way to sample the delights of Singapore.

Before you sign up for a tour be clear about what the tour offers – a lot of brochures will list tourist attractions as features of the tour, but find out if you'll actually be visiting these places or whether you'll simply be looking at them through the window of a fast-moving minibus. Many tourist operators run tours to major attractions, such as the zoo or the Jurong Bird Park: find out what value they add above the usual admission.

The Singapore Tourist Bureau (STB) at Suntec City (#01-35 Suntec City, 3 Temasek Blvd;

> ### Tour Agencies
> A number of the tours listed here are run by more than one tour operator. Contact any of the following to book one of these tours:
> - **Ananda Travel**; #03-05/08, 15 Scotts Rd; 4, A4; ☎ 6732 1766; Ⓜ Orchard
> - **Holiday Tours & Travel**; #07-01/10 The Promenade, 300 Orchard Rd; 4, C6; ☎ 6738 2622; Ⓜ Orchard
> - **RMG Tours**; 109C Amoy St; 3, M5; ☎ 6220 1661; Ⓜ Raffles Place
> - **SH Tours**; #02-02/03, 100 Kim Seng Plaza, 100 Kim Seng Rd; 3, H1; ☎ 6734 9923, 🚌 75, 195, 970
> - **Singapore Sightseeing Tour East**; #01-24/25, 3C River Valley Rd, Cannery Block, Clarke Quay; 3, J4; ☎ 6332 3755, 🚌 65, 139, 970

☎ 1800 332 5066; 8am-6.30pm) can book tours for you. Most companies will pick up from hotels or will offer a centrally located meeting point.

In addition to the walking tours earlier this chapter the STB publishes several free brochures detailing self-guided walks around popular areas.

Travel agents in Singapore offer a host of package tours to neighbouring Malaysia and Indonesia and the fierce competition results in some good deals. For suggestions, ask your hotel, the STB or check *The Straits Times* for advertisements.

Tour the zoo to catch these birds of a feather.

Academy at-sunrice: Singapore Cooking School and Spice Garden (3, G5)

Tour the Fort Canning Spice Garden and put your new knowledge into action with a spice-making session and cooking class or high tea.
✉ **Fort Canning Centre, Cox Terrace** ☎ **6336 3307** Ⓜ **Dhoby Ghaut** ⏰ **walk 8.30am, demonstration 10am, cooking class 11.30am; walk & high tea Tues, Thur & Sat 5-7pm** ⑤ **$20, $30, $50, $75 depending on tour**

Asian Culinary Tours

Explore the sights, smells and tastes of Singapore's rich culinary heritage with visits to the Fort Canning Spice Garden, wet markets, Little India spice shops and herbal medical halls in Chinatown.
Book through agencies listed opposite ⏰ **Mon-Sat approx 8am, approx 3½hrs** ⑤ **$28/15**

Eastwind Harbour Cruises (3, L7)

Offers 1-2½hr daytime, sunset and evening cruises around Singapore's islands (Brani, Lazarus, St John's) aboard an old Chinese junk with stopoffs on Kusu Island (except at festival time).
✉ **#01-30A Clifford Pier, 70 Collyer Quay** ☎ **6533 3432** Ⓜ **Raffles Place** ⏰ **10.30am, 3pm, 4pm & 6pm** ⑤ **$20/10 or $36/18 with buffet dinner**

Feng Shui Tours

The ancient art of geomancy underlies much of the planning of Singapore's buildings both new and old. The 3½hr tour takes in a trip to a feng

shui gallery and Suntec City.
Book through agencies listed opposite ⏰ **Mon-Fri approx 1pm** ⑤ **$33/17**

Nature Tours

This local guide organises private hiking, bird-watching and nature tours to Pulau Ubin, Bukit Timah, Johor and further afield on request. Prices vary according to group size, tour complexity and equipment required (eg, boats, bikes).
☎ **6787 4733** 🄴 **serin@swiftech .com.sg** ⑤ **$30+**

Painted Faces (Chinese Opera)

This 3½hr evening tour begins at a traditional Chinese opera props-and-costume shop and includes an explanation of traditional opera and make-up techniques followed by an opera performance.
Book through agencies listed opposite ⑤ **$53/27 includes dinner & opera**

Registered Tourist Guides Association

Offers personalised tours by registered guides ranging from the concrete jungle to the great outdoors.
☎ **6339 2114** ⑤ **varies**

SIA Hop-On

A great way to see the city without transport headaches; visit Merlion Park, Boat Quay, Chinatown, Singapore Botanical Gardens, Orchard Rd and others. Hop on and off as you like.
Main stops are in front of Suntec City (3 Temasek Blvd), Orchard Hotel (442 Orchard Rd), Le Meridien hotel (Orchard Rd) and Sri Mariamman

Temple (South Bridge Rd) ☎ **9457 2965** ⏰ **8am-5pm** ⑤ **$6/4 day pass, $3 with Singapore Airlines or SilkAir boarding pass.**

Singapore by Night

Offers a tame and somewhat cliched 3½hr tour of Singapore nightlife. Includes dinner at Boat Quay, the laser show at the Fountain of Wealth (see p. 46) and peanut throwing and Singapore Slings at Raffles.
Book through agencies listed opposite ⏰ **6pm** ⑤ **$43-54/22-32**

Singapore River (3, L6)

Several tour operators offer tours of the river's historical sites with or without high tea and buffet dinners. Or you can tour it yourself by catching a water taxi from Boat Quay jetty.
Book through agencies listed opposite ⑤ **water taxi $3/2, tours $20/10+**

Singapore Turf Club (2, B6)

Take in 4hrs of horse racing under floodlights from the cool, air-conditioned Club level grandstand, which offers refreshments and private betting counters.
Book through agencies listed opposite ⏰ **approx 5.30pm** ⑤ **$45 (adults only)**

Trishaws (3, F7)

Sit back and relax through the streets of Little India and Chinatown on these nifty three-wheelers. You'll find drivers at Bugis Village.
✉ **Bugis Village (cnr Rocher Rd & Victoria St)** Ⓜ **Bugis** ⑤ **$30-40 for 45mins**

shopping

Shopping (along with eating and movie-going) is among Singaporeans' three favourite pastimes. Orchard Rd offers unrivalled opportunities to spend your life's savings without moving more than 20m in any direction, but window shopping is free. It can also be fun to explore small businesses in the backstreets of Chinatown, Little India and around Arab St.

Prices & Bargaining

Compared to neighbouring countries Singapore is no bargain hunter's paradise and you may find that prices are equal to those at home. Prices are usually fixed except at markets and in touristy areas. If you do have to bargain stay good-humoured and don't get petty – this causes everyone to lose face. Also, don't start a bargaining session if you have no real interest in buying.

Problems

When buying electronic goods make sure they have an international guarantee. Singapore enforces international copyright laws and you are not likely to be palmed off with pirated goods,

Kiasu & the Hello Kitty Riots

A Hokkien concept meaning 'afraid to lose', *kiasu* entered Singapore's popular lexicon via the Mr Kiasu cartoon character whose philosophy is to win at all costs. Kiasu behaviour includes jumping queues, gorging at buffet dinners and bargaining hard. Despite the government's ongoing anti-kiasu-behaviour campaigns kiasu is a retailer's deadliest marketing tool. Advertising a FOC (free of charge) shopper gift or 'limited edition' goods is guaranteed to swell the traffic of Orchard Rd. Kiasu madness reached its height in 2000 when shoppers exchanged blows after queuing for days to buy 'limited edition' Hello Kittys from McDonalds.

but if you do purchase pirated goods you may find yourself in trouble with customs officials. If you have any serious problems with a retailer you can contact the Singapore Tourism Board (STB) or the Small Claims Tribunal (☎ 435 5946, fax 451 4207); tourist complaints are usually heard within two or three days. You can access the tribunal's website through [e] www.gov.sg.

GST

Almost all goods and services are levied with a 3% goods and services tax (GST). A tax refund on goods worth $300 or more can be applied for through shops participating in the GST Tourist Refund Scheme. These shops will display a 'tax-free shopping' logo, though often it's more hassle than it's worth.

Great Singapore Sale

In an effort to reverse Singapore's declining image as a bargain hunter's destination, the STB and Orchard Rd traders promote the Great Singapore Sale, held every year in July.

DEPARTMENT STORES

Eu Hwa Chinese Products (3, N2)
This five-storey building stocks everything Chinese, from porcelain teapots and jade jewellery to slinky silk cheongsams, dried fish and medicinal herbs.
✉ 70 Eu Tong Sen St
☎ 6538 4222
🚍 63, 124, 174, 197
🕐 10.30am-9pm

Dress to impress.

Funan IT Mall (3, J5)
Here you'll find hardware, software and everything in between at competitive prices. If you're dazzled by choice try **Challenger Superstore** up top.
✉ 109 North Bridge Rd

☎ 6337 4235 🚇 Bugis
🕐 10.30am-9pm

Hilton Shopping Gallery (4, C3)
If Orchard Rd isn't burning your dollars fast enough try giving some of it away to the guys at Issey Miyake, Paul Smith, Fendi, Club 21, Moschino and Gucci.
✉ Hilton Hotel, 581 Orchard Rd ☎ 6737 2233 🚇 Orchard
🕐 10.30am-6pm

Isetan Department Store (4, C4)
Everything you could ever need and heaps of stuff you don't. Big brands include Agnes B, Laura Ashley and Polo Ralph Lauren.
✉ Shaw House, 350 Orchard Rd ☎ 733 1111 🚇 Orchard
🕐 10.30am-9pm

Sim Lim Square
(3, E7) Computer, video, camera and electronic equipment stores crowd each other on the ground floor. Be prepared to bar-

gain hard.
✉ 1 Rochor Canal Rd
☎ 6332 5839 🚇 Bugis
🚍 65, 97, 103, 106
🕐 10.30am-9pm

Takashimaya Shopping Centre
(4, C6) Huge Japanese department store with handy maps in English and Japanese, stocking everything from foot reflexology products to pianos. Facilities include kid-friendly bathrooms (level 3), post office (level 4) and an alterations service (level 3).
✉ Ngee Ann City, 391 Orchard Rd ☎ 6733 0337 🚇 Somerset, Orchard 🚍 7, 65, 106, 124, 167, 174
🕐 10am-9.30pm

Tangs (4, C5)
This monstrous, home-grown brand housed in an Oriental-look mall started out as a small family business; it offers regular sales.
✉ 320 Orchard Rd
☎ 6737 550
🚇 Orchard
🕐 10.30am-9pm

Department store dreams come true on Orchard Rd.

LOCAL DESIGNERS & BOUTIQUES

Belle (4, B5)
Catering to the bright and the beautiful, the artfully designed Belle stocks clothes, shoes, bags and trinkets by William Reid, Wink, Ana Sui and Marc Jacobs. Local designers include Cat in the Bag and Mian.
✉ **Shop 1, Main Lobby, Grand Hyatt, 10-12 Scotts Rd** ☎ **6736 0483** Ⓜ **Orchard**
🕙 **11am-8pm**

Calypso (4, B4)
The shop's already looking a little rough around the edges (cat fight over a markdown?) but Calypso is proving itself a hit with the in-crowd who are lining up to purchase girly wisps of Colette.
✉ **#02-17 Pacific Plaza, 9 Scotts Rd** ☎ **6736 0620** Ⓜ **Orchard**
🕙 **11am-8pm**

Centro (4, C7)
Get glam-trashy and retro-ironic at Centro, which stocks quirky streetwear of the kind favoured by young Singaporean funksters, funkettes and street-press fashion editors. Clothes hang from monkey-bar-style hangers.
✉ **#02-01 The Heeren, 260 Orchard Rd**
☎ **6733 8202**
Ⓜ **Somerset**
🕙 **11.30am-8.30pm**

Dressing Room (3, M4) Perfect for dancing queens, here you'll find studded, disco T-shirts, swinging silver chain belts and nifty pants all in little men's sizes. The boutique shares approximately the same opening hours as the men's Backstage Bar (p. 98).
✉ **13A Trengganu St**
☎ **6221 2044**
Ⓜ **Outram Park**
🕙 **approx 7am-2am**

EPO (3, F7)
Extreme, Practical, Outrageous wear. Cute shop stocking tiny vacuum-wrapped Ts in sweet colours with rebel slogans and snazzy sneakers.
✉ **#02-39 Parco Bugis Junction, 200 Victoria St**
☎ **6338 9120** Ⓜ **Bugis**
🕙 **11am-9pm**

Flag (3, F7)
Flag designer Alfie has found a niche in Singapore's fashion fringe. Expect arty cuts and androgynous 1980s-inspired looks in surprisingly heavy fabrics.
✉ **#01-34 Parco Bugis Junction, 200 Victoria St** ☎ **6338 8535**
Ⓜ **Bugis**
🕙 **10.30am-9.30pm**

Ab Fab

In March the annual Singapore Fashion Festival showcases international, regional and local designers at ticketed or free indoor or street parades. Check this website for details: ⓔ www.fashion-festival.com, or ask at the STB for more information.

The Heeren, Levels 4 & 5 (4, C7)
Work your way up the Heeren's escalator to a labyrinth of anarchic fashionistas selling home-grown creations and avant-garde rip-offs out of micro-sized boutiques. Our favourites include Day Tripper, Opt Shop, Clothes Matter and the intriguingly named Fourskin (for boys!). Bring ear plugs and coins for the video game parlour.
✉ **#02-01 The Heeren, 260 Orchard Rd**
☎ **6733 4725**
Ⓜ **Somerset** 🕙 **approx 10.30am-10pm**

Malebox (4, B4)
This trendy men's store is decked out in wood and

This one's in the bag.

leather and stocks quality leather shoes by Johnston & Murphy (USA), Passport (Italy) and Malaysian brand Lewre. Prices hover from $50 to $500 and service includes fashion advice and style assessment – no more fashion disasters!
✉ **#02-09 Pacific Plaza, 9 Scotts Rd** ☎ 6733 5655 Ⓜ **Orchard**
🕑 **11am-8pm**

M)phosis (4, C6)

Miniature wisps of girly, slinky, sexy bits and pieces by local designer Colin Koh. You may increase your chances of actually fitting into something if you buy two pieces and sew them together. You'll also find a branch at Parco Bugis Junction.
✉ **#B1-09/10 Ngee Ann City, 391 Orchard Rd** ☎ 6737 6539 Ⓜ **Orchard, Somerset** 🚌 **7, 65, 106, 124, 167, 174** 🕑 **11am-9pm**

POA People of Asia

(3, F7) Skate looks for the boys and 'I'm cute but quirky' items for the girls. Expect street press on the sales counter and amusing sales assistants who may or may not be rocking to the in-store CD collection at maximum volume.
✉ **#02-10 Parco Bugis Junction, 200 Victoria St**

☎ **6333 4582** Ⓜ **Bugis**
🕑 **10am-9pm**

Pois Boutique (4, B6)

Lingerie and feminine frippery by European labels including Jiki, Hervé Leger, Cipher (Poland), Jorando (Italy) and Ghost (London).
✉ **#02-19 The Paragon, 290 Orchard Rd**
☎ **6238 0151**
Ⓜ **Orchard**
🕑 **11am-7pm**

Project Shop Blood Brothers (4, C6)

Sexy streetwear – tank tops, cute T-shirts and tiny sun dresses all in pre-pubescent sizes.
✉ **#02-09 Ngee Ann City, 391 Orchard Rd**
☎ **6737 8058**
Ⓜ **Orchard, Somerset**
🚌 **7, 65, 106, 124, 167, 174** 🕑 **11am-9pm**

Song+Kelly21 (4, C3)

Here at Wykidd Song and Ann Kelly's retail outlet you'll find sleek, slick, feminine designs and nothing too outrageous. They also stock Dr Hauscka beauty products and homewares by the Danish company Stelton.
✉ **#01-38 Forum Galleria, 583 Orchard Rd**
☎ **6735 3387**
Ⓜ **Orchard** 🕑 **Mon-Sat 10.30am-7.30pm, Sun 11am-6pm**

Surf Diva (4, B4)

Itsy, bitsy bikinis by Aussie surf brands Silverwear and Beachwear, in a teensy pink boutique.
✉ **#03-16 Pacific Plaza, 9 Scotts Rd** ☎ 6735 8835 Ⓜ **Orchard**
🕑 **Mon-Fri 10.30am-8.30pm, Sat noon-8pm, Sun 12.30-7pm**

Itsy bitsy teeny weeny…

Time Engine (3, F7)

Here's something for the boys: chunky stainless-steel jewellery, Swiss timepieces and executive bibs and bobs by Christian Kraus sold from a gunmetal steel trap.
✉ **#01-13 Parco Bugis Junction, 200 Victoria St**
☎ **6883 0833** Ⓜ **Bugis**
🕑 **11am-8pm**

Woods & Woods

(4, B4) Stylish store stocking products from Singapore designers Woods & Woods: gorgeous felts, fine linens – minimal, somewhat androgynous designs with artsy cuts catering for the well-dressed, individualistic pretty boy and girl.
✉ **#02-16 Pacific Plaza, 9 Scotts Rd** ☎ 6887 5054 Ⓜ **Orchard**
🕑 **noon-9pm**

Face up to fashion: shopping is a national pastime.

BLOCKBUSTER BRANDS

Birkenstock (4, D1)
A million German back-packers can't be wrong. This shop has a range of styles and sizes of the famous sandal (including tots'), ideally worn with socks.
✉ **#02-27 Tanglin Mall, 163 Tanglin Rd** ☎ **6835 2702** 🚌 **7, 77, 106, 111, 123, 132, 174** ⏱ **11am-9pm**

Burberry (4, C6)
Waif-sized Japanese girls stock up on extra-small everything for that top-to-toe all-over Burberry-print raincoat look. Alas, no pooch wear on display.
✉ **#01-28/29 Takashimaya, Ngee Ann City, 391 Orchard Rd** ☎ **6735 1283** Ⓜ **Orchard, Somerset** 🚌 **7, 65, 106, 124, 167, 174** ⏱ **10am-9pm**

Emporio Armani
(4, C3) The Emporio stocks men's and women's Armani-everything, from evening to casual to sports and underwear, so theoretically you could walk in naked – but don't forget your wallet.
✉ **#01-01 Forum Galleria, 583 Orchard Rd** ☎ **6734 5766** Ⓜ **Orchard** ⏱ **Mon-Sat 10am-8pm, Sun 11am-6.30pm**

Helmut Lang (4, B4)
Spacious, stark and dra-matic, Helmut Lang's Singapore branch outsizes those in Tokyo and Hong Kong. It stocks the usual men's and women's shoes and clothing in pure shades of – you guessed it – black, white and grey.
✉ **#02-10/11/12/13**

Pacific Plaza, 9 Scotts Rd ☎ **6736 2954** Ⓜ **Orchard** ⏱ **Mon-Sat 10.30am-8pm, Sun 10.30am-7.30pm**

Louis Vuitton (4, C6)
Check out the window dis-play – as if you could miss it. Inside badly dressed IT geeks and business moguls loll around on couches egoising, but quietly sweat-ing while their wives pick out something gorgeously expensive. Flip-flops are a steal at $500.
✉ **ground fl, Takashimaya, Ngee Ann City, 391 Orchard Rd** ☎ **6734 7760** Ⓜ **Orchard, Somerset** 🚌 **7, 65, 106, 124, 167, 174** ⏱ **10.30am-9pm**

Prada (4, B3)
Where else in Singapore will you find cute sales boys in black turtlenecks? Of course, the clothes aren't bad either – especially if you're spend-ing someone else's money.
✉ **#01-01/02 Palais Renaissance, 390 Orchard Rd** ☎ **6737 1520** Ⓜ **Orchard** ⏱ **Mon-Sat 10am-8pm, Sun 11am-6pm**

Stussy (4, B4)
Here's skate wear, surf wear and streetwear for teens and adults who aren't quite ready to grow up yet.
✉ **#01-07/08 Pacific**

Plaza, 9 Scotts Rd ☎ **6738 2270** Ⓜ **Orchard** ⏱ **Mon-Sat 11am-9pm, Sun 11am-7.30pm**

The Link Men (4, B3)
This is an upmarket menswear store stocking the cool and interesting. Dashing ties, snazzy cuff-links and groovy shirts for the man about town.
✉ **#02-10/11 Palais Renaissance, 390 Orchard Rd** ☎ **6733 7185** Ⓜ **Orchard** ⏱ **Mon-Sat 10.30am-7pm, Sun 1-6pm**

Timberland (4, B9)
Everything the big urban man needs to feel like a big outdoorsy kind of guy. Shoes also come in kiddie sizes.
✉ **#01-09/13 Centrepoint, 176 Orchard Rd** ☎ **6735 9050** Ⓜ **Somerset, Dhoby Ghaut** ⏱ **10.30am-9.30pm**

Versace (4, B3)
Ah...the glamour, the pas-sion, the intrigue, the filthy riches. Dress to kill at Versace. Sadly the interior falls short of over-the-top but at least it's trying.
✉ **#02 Palais Renaissance, 390 Orchard Rd** ☎ **6734 6318** Ⓜ **Orchard** ⏱ **Mon-Sat 10am-8pm, Sun 11am-6pm**

For those with a passion for fashion.

FOOD & DRINK

In addition to these speciality stores you can try the **Chinatown Complex** (3, M4) in Chinatown and **Tekka Centre** (3, D6) in Little India for market supplies, otherwise you'll find a supermarkets at **Tanglin Mall Food Junction** in the Tanglin Mall (4, D1), a branch of **Carrefour** in Suntec City mall (3, H8) and **Cold Storage** in Holland Village (2, F7).

A Jaffar Spices Centre (3, D6)
Here you can take away big bags of chilli, turmeric, cumin or fennel or order them by the scoop. Or check out the traditional spice-grinding shop on Cuff Rd off Serangoon Rd (open Tues-Sun 9am-6.30pm).
✉ **#01-69 Campbell Block, Little India Arcade, 48 Serangoon Rd** ☎ 6294 4833
🚌 65, 97, 103, 106
🕐 10am-10pm

Brown Rice Paradise (4, D1) This place stocks fresh, dried and processed organic and natural foods including baby food, Asian groceries and a small selection of potentially drinkable organic wines.
✉ **#03-15/16 Tanglin Mall, 163 Tanglin Rd** ☎ 6738 1121 🚌 7, 77, 106, 111, 123, 132, 174 🕐 Mon-Fri 9.30am-9pm, Sat-Sun 10.30am-9pm

Chwee Hin Trading (3, M4) Low-key Chinese bakery selling all the old favourites: sweet red and yellow bean cakes, moon cakes and peanut biscuits. Be prepared to queue, this place attracts crowds!
✉ **#01-34 Sago St**
🚇 **Raffles Place**
🕐 8am-5pm

Gainswell Trading (3, M4) You can never have too much dried abalone on hand. Here's where you can stock up on everything to please the fussiest of guests: chocolate bubble tea mix, wild ginseng and whole or grated saiga antelope horn.
✉ **54 Smith St**
☎ 6324 8283
🚇 **Raffles Place**
🕐 9am-8pm

Komala Vilas Sweet Shop (3, D6)
Multi-coloured milky, sugary Indian sweets with edible silver and gold foil wrappers – pick up a bunch to take away.
✉ **76-78 Serangoon Rd** ☎ 6293 6990
🚌 65, 97, 103, 106
🕐 11am-9.30pm

Teaspa (3, H7)
Teaspa is a slick tea boutique and cafe specialising in black and Chinese teas and DIY herbal blends; try mixing ginseng, lavender or fennel into your favourite blend.
✉ **#03-21C Raffles**

City, **252 North Bridge Rd** ☎ 6425 3520
🚇 **City Hall**
🕐 noon-9.30pm

Thossb (3, H7)
This gourmet shop in the Raffles complex stocks fine teas, chutneys, genuine smelly cheeses and a superb range of upmarket wines at surprisingly reasonable prices.
✉ **#01-30/31 Raffles Hotel Arcade, 328 North Bridge Rd** ☎ 6421 1148 🚇 **City Hall**
🕐 8.30am-8.30pm

The Vintner (4, B3)
When a thirst strikes this tiny wine shop is stacked floor to ceiling with the good stuff from such famed wine-producing countries as Australia, France, Italy and South Africa.
✉ **#02-30 Orchard Towers, 400 Orchard Rd** ☎ 6235 2784
🚇 **Orchard**
🕐 Mon-Fri 11am-7pm, Sat 11am-4.30pm

Sweet Talk

Burfi, ladoo, gulab jamun, gelabi, jangiri, kesari and *halwa*! Is this the sound of someone trying to talk with their mouth full, or the names of Little India's most popular sweets? Rot your teeth on technicolour milky offerings complete with edible foil, available along Serangoon Rd and in the Little India Arcade (3, D6).

ARTS, CRAFTS, HOMEWARE & ANTIQUES

Ansa Store (3, D6)

Here you can pick up a freshly carved wooden picture frame or table, but the draw-cards are the wildly coloured posters and pictures of religious icons. A poster of Krishna will cost around $10.

✉ 29 Kerbau Rd
☎ 6295 6605
🚌 65, 97, 103, 106
🕐 10.30am-9pm

Avid (5, D5)

Avid is a groovy, interior-designer-run store stocking restored vintage and locally designed pop art and furnishings. Choose from retro wall hangings, clunky clocks and outrageous, 1960s spinning ball chairs – great for devising fiendish schemes when you return home.

✉ #01-08, 252 Tembeling Rd ☎ 6348 3208 🕐 11am-8pm

Chic to Chic (4, D1)

This place is ideal for buying small but pretty things for friends back home. Stock includes woven straw bags from the Philippines, linens from Indonesia, silk shawls from Thailand and Celadon pottery from China.

✉ #02-32-33 Tanglin

Mall, 163 Tanglin Rd
☎ 6737 9228 🚌 7, 77, 106, 111, 123, 132, 174 🕐 10.30am-10pm

Gary Lee (3, M4)

This shop stocks delicate new and antique hand-embroidered handkerchiefs, tablecloths and bed sets of Chinese, Swiss and Belgium cotton, linen and organza, all imported from China.

✉ 20 Smith St ☎ 6221 8129 🕐 Mon-Sat 11am-7pm, Sun 12.30-7pm

Hassan's Carpets

(4, C2) These guys have been in the carpet business since the 1930s and they still offer one of the largest collections of antique carpets in the region. Carpets can be custom made but making and delivery can take up to six months.

✉ #03-01/06 Tanglin Shopping Centre, 19 Tanglin Rd ☎ 6737 5626 🚌 7, 77, 106, 111, 123, 132, 174 🕐 Mon-Sat 10am-7pm, Sun 11am-4pm

Heritage Shop (3, M4)

Singaporean kitsch – where else in Singapore

can you pick up vintage postcards, 1960s Canto pop LPs, old posters of cigarette girls or a framed photograph of Mao?

✉ 25 Erskine Rd
☎ 6223 7982
Ⓜ Raffles Place
🕐 noon-8pm

Katong Antique House (5, D5)

A dusty and slightly musty old shophouse packed high with old Peranakan goodies and quite a bit of trash – worth having a fossick through.

✉ 208 East Coast Rd
☎ 6345 8544 🕐 Mon-Sat by appointment

Lajeunesse Asian Art

(3, M4) This shop features posh art, Asian furniture and objects 'chosen for their beauty and power to inspire'. You can expect to find gold leaf Buddhist statues, wooden screens, replica religious reliefs and chic chopsticks.

✉ 94 Club St ☎ 6224 7975 Ⓜ Raffles Place 🕐 Mon-Sat 11am-7pm

Nalli (3, D6)

This is a fine spot for traditional Indian silk and gold thread sari fabric and traditional blouses. A deluxe sari costs from around $200 to $1000 for the mega-show-off variety. Alternatively you could buy the material and have them whip up a skirt for you.

✉ 27 Campbell Lane
☎ 6334 0341
🚌 65, 97, 103, 106
🕐 9.30am-9pm

Neutral Art (3, M4)

This design-studio-cum-gallery specialises in groovy

Fine Asian art and furniture at Lajeunesse.

lights cleverly fashioned from surprising elements such as recycled film canisters, plastic tubes and old tin cans.

✉ **50 Temple St**
☎ **6227 2690**
Ⓜ **Raffles Place**
🕐 **by appointment**

Paras Pashmina Arts

(3, M4) Prepare to bargain hard (but nicely!) for pashminas or beautiful handmade antique blankets from Rajasthan, India.

✉ **#01-01A, 20 Trengganu St** ☎ **6224 4850** Ⓜ **Raffles Place**
🕐 **9am-7.30pm**

Red Peach Gallery

(3, L4) This upmarket gallery stocks posh and decorative homewares with an Asiatic vibe. Faves include raw silk cushion covers, nifty cutlery sets and odd Chinese teapots.

✉ **68 Pagoda St**
☎ **6222 2215**
Ⓜ **Raffles Place**
🕐 **10.30am-7pm**

Shing's Antique Gallery (3, M4)

One of the better options along the tourist strip in Chinatown, featuring furnishings old and new from China. Head on down to check out the beautiful wooden screens and antique window grills.

✉ **24A & 26 Pagoda St**
☎ **6224 4332**
Ⓜ **Raffles Place**
🕐 **10am-7pm**

Tanglin Shopping Centre (4, C2)

Probably the best place for antiques in Singapore. You'll find antique carpets, wall hangings, artwork, cabinets and all manner of trinkets spread over several floors. Bargaining is expected.

✉ **19 Tanglin Rd**
☎ **6732 8751**
🚌 **7, 77, 106, 111, 123, 132, 174** 🕐 **Mon-Sat approx 11am-7pm, Sun 11am-4pm**

Thow's Gallery

(3, M4) This small, crowded shop specialises in Chinese antiques (black-

wood, bronze, porcelain and jade) from the Neolithic age to the Ching dynasty – though we're not sure how you're going to lift that giant lump of jade into the overhead locker.

✉ **63 Temple St**
☎ **6324 6711**
Ⓜ **Raffles Place**
🕐 **10am-5pm**

Zhen Lacquer Gallery

(3, M4) This souvenir shop stocks pretty things from all over South-East Asia, specialising in Vietnamese lacquer ware. Pick up a mother-of-pearl jewellery box, a mah jong set or an antique Chinese embroidery featuring the 'forbidden stitch' – so named because it's so miniscule that women lost their eyesight as a result of sewing. Tiny Chinese women's bound-feet shoes are also for sale.

✉ **1 Trengganu St**
☎ **6222 2718**
Ⓜ **Raffles Place**
🕐 **9.30am-6.30pm**

Don't head home without one!

MUSIC & BOOKS

Audiosports Proshop
(4, C7) Here's everything you need to make it as a professional DJ – except an audience. There's a small selection of vinyl and hugely expensive but impressive-looking DJ gadgetry and turntables by Vestax. Set yourself up in the living room and go crazy.
✉ #04-11 The Heeren, 260 Orchard Rd ☎ 6834 9133 Ⓜ Somerset ⏰ 11am-9.30pm

Borders (4, C4)
These guys are overtaking the world. Expect the usual Borders fare, including CDs and a great range of inter-national magazines, regional newspapers, travel books and local literature. There's a coffee shop out front.
✉ #01-00 Wheelock Pl, 501 Orchard Rd ☎ 6235 7146 (books), 6235 9113 (music) Ⓜ Orchard ⏰ Sun-Thur 9am-11pm, Fri-Sat 9am-midnight

HMV (4, C7)
HMV boasts three humungous floors of CDs, vinyl, mags and music-induced mayhem. Check out the in-house DJ. There's a good regional selection from Singapore, Hong Kong and Japan.
✉ #01-11 The Heeren, 260 Orchard Rd ☎ 6733 1822 Ⓜ Somerset ⏰ 10am-11pm

Indian Classical Music Centre (3, D6)
This store has a small but ample supply of everything the aspiring Sergeant Pepper needs to get into that Hindustani beat: sitar, tabla, bells – wearable and shakeable – and CDs.
✉ #01-29 Hastings Block, Little India Arcade, 48 Serangoon Rd ☎ 6291 0187 🚌 65, 97, 103, 106 ⏰ Mon-Sat 10am-8pm, Sun 10am-4pm

Kinokuniya (4, C6)
This place claims to be the biggest bookshop in all South-East Asia – and it is true you could get lost in here for days (pack emer-gency rations!). There's a friendly kids' reading section where most of the books are already strewn across the floor so you can relax. It's also worth checking out the local literature section.
✉ #03-10/15 391 Ngee Ann City, 391 Orchard Rd ☎ 6737 5021 Ⓜ Orchard, Somerset 🚌 7, 65, 106, 124, 167, 174 ⏰ 10.30am-9pm

MPH Books (3, H6)
In a historic building that's been home to publishing since 1908 – not that you'd guess from the refurbished interior – MPH boasts a cafe and a good selection of travel and business books.
✉ MPH Building, 71/77 Stamford Rd ☎ 6336 3633 Ⓜ City Hall ⏰ 10am-9pm; cafe 10.30am-9pm

Bookworms
Great local fiction includes award-winning plays *The Coffin is Too Big for the Hole* by Kuo Pao Kun and *Emily of Emerald Hill*, about the archetypal Nonya (Peranakan) matriarch; *Little Ironies*, short stories by Catherine Lim, and the satirical novel *Mammon Inc* by Gen-Xer Hwee Hwee Tan. Poetry includes Landmark Books' *One Fierce Hour*. For popular raves see X'Ho's *Skew Me You Rebel Meh? Thoughts of a Disavowed Rebel in Singapore* (see p. 100). For politics try the hefty tome *Singapore Story: Memoirs of Lee Kuan Yew*, or the contemporary and readable *Singapore: The Air-Conditioned Nation* by Cherian George. War buffs should see *King Rat* by James Clavell; long-term visitors might try *Culture Shock Singapore!* by Time Books.

Sunny Books (4, A5)
This is the spot for second-hand books – just a stone's throw from the glitz of Orchard Rd.
✉ **#03-58/59 Far East Plaza, 14 Scotts Rd**
☎ **6733 1583**
Ⓜ **Orchard**
🕐 10.30am-8pm

That CD Shop (4, D1)
Organised like a floor-to-ceiling CD display rack this store specialises in jazz, acid jazz and French house and is easy to navigate. If you're throwing a party

the staff are happy to play you suggestions.
✉ **#01-17/18/19/20 Tanglin Mall, 163 Tanglin Rd** ☎ **6732 2568** 🚌 **7, 77, 106, 111, 123, 132, 174**
🕐 10am-10pm

Tower Records (3, H8)
As well as the usual pop and rock, this big, mainstream record store features separate rooms for Asian and classical music plus a cafe.
✉ **#02-063/065/067 Suntec City, 3 Temasek Blvd** ☎ **6735 5755**

Ⓜ **City Hall**
🚌 **97, 124, 167, 174**
🕐 **Sun-Thur 10am-10pm, Fri-Sat 10am-11pm**

V & V Music Centre (3, D7) Indian ex-pats flock here for the latest Subcontinental hits, but Bollywood soundtracks remain the steady favourite. Mix 'em up for a musical extravaganza at home.
✉ **144 Dunlop St**
☎ **6927 6467**
🚌 **65, 97, 103, 106**
🕐 11am-10pm

FOR CHILDREN

You'll find a host of children's shops at Suntec City mall (3, H8), the Tanglin Shopping Centre (4, C2) and the Forum Galleria (4, C3). And if you and your young 'uns want to browse for books, check out Kinokuniya's friendly kids' area (p. 70; 4, C6).

Forum Galleria (4, C3)
If you're wise you'll ban the kids from this shopping mall. It's packed with munchkin-sized designer brat-wear selling at adult prices. If you want to ruin them forever you'll also find a big Toys R Us on the third floor.
✉ **583 Orchard Rd**
☎ **6732 2479**
Ⓜ **Orchard**
🕐 10.30am-9pm

Mothercare (3, H8)
Stocking the usual baby equipment, Mothercare also has several other branches in Singapore including: Centrepoint (#01-34/39; 4, B9) and Marina Square (#02-100; 3, J8).
✉ **#02-003/5/7 Suntec City, 3 Temasek Blvd**
☎ **6337 0388**
Ⓜ **City Hall** 🚌 **97, 124, 167, 174**
🕐 11.30am-9pm

Nurture Craft (3, H8)
Specialising in educational toys, stock ranges from puzzles and science experiments to books with inspiring titles, like *Spelling is Fun!* But will the kids fall for it?
✉ **#02-044 Suntec City, 3 Temasek Blvd**
☎ **6336 8717** Ⓜ **City Hall** 🚌 **97, 124, 167, 174** 🕐 11am-8pm

Petite Cherie Boutique (3, H8)
This small shoe shop stocks a reasonable range of trendy, well-made kids' shoes by European brands.
✉ **#02-043 Suntec City, 3 Temasek Blvd**
☎ **6821 3668** Ⓜ **City Hall** 🚌 **97, 124, 167, 174** 🕐 10.30am-9pm

Samsui Shop (3, H6)
This tiny store is crammed

with soft hand-sewn toys and dolls inspired by the Samsui women – the construction workers who immigrated to Singapore in the 1930s and '40s.
✉ **#01-15 Chijmes, 30 Victoria St** ☎ **6332 5488** Ⓜ **City Hall**
🕐 11am-6pm

Kid-Sized Prices

Children under 90cm in height may be eligible for extra discounts and free travel. If you need to make some savings consider chopping their legs off.

SPECIALIST STORES

Action City (4, C7)
In *kiasu*-conscious Singapore it always pays to have the latest thing. This store stocks a good range of models and figures for collectors and hobbyists. Right now the coolest things are the tiny street-wise Hong Kong gong zai action figures based on the *Gardener* cartoon strip designed by cartoonist and sometime Levis model Michael Lau.
✉ #05-2/3 The Heeren, 260 Orchard Rd ☎ 6738 7253 Ⓜ Somerset ◷ 11.30am-10pm

Crazy Condoms
(4, B3) When the ordinary kind just won't do the job. Go local with the durian special or try for a jungle vibe with an elephant strap-on.
✉ #01-14 Orchard Towers, 400 Orchard Rd ☎ 6734 5902 Ⓜ Orchard ◷ Mon-Thur noon-11pm, Fri-Sat 1pm-1am

Manchester United
(4, B2) Singapore is teeming with football fans – here's your chance to connect with like minds through gratuitous consumption. Why not stock up on Manchester United mugs, slippers, Monopoly or lamps? Football games are sometimes screened in the bar upstairs (open Mon-Fri noon-8pm, Sat-Sun noon-4pm; over 18 years only).
✉ #01-01 Orchard Parade Hotel, 1 Tanglin Rd ☎ 6732 6266 🚌 7, 77, 106, 111, 123, 132, 174 ◷ Mon-Fri 11am-9pm, Sat-Sun 11am-10pm

Nam's Supplies
(3, M4) This store is stocked top to bottom with bright technicolour packages of incense sticks and coils. The joss paper is popular with tourists (ideal as arty notepaper) but locals stop in for ancestral offerings – paper versions of real things that a Singaporean would need in the afterlife, such as a nice suit, gold watch and a mobile phone.
✉ 22 Smith St ☎ 6324 5872 Ⓜ Raffles Place ◷ 7.30am-8pm

Ordning & Reda
(3, J7) Stylish Swedish stationery chain selling great notepaper, nifty DIY photo albums and really expensive staplers – all in simple, eye-catching primary colours.
✉ #B1-53 CityLink Mall, 1 Raffles Link ☎ 6423 1231 Ⓜ City Hall ◷ 10am-9pm

SNG Arms (3, M4)
Singapore's not exactly an outdoorsy kind of place, but here's somewhere you can stock up on basics like mosquito nets, water bottles and water purification tablets before you hit the road.
✉ 9 Trengganu St ☎ 6223 3966 Ⓜ Raffles Place ◷ 9am-10pm

The Oaks (4, D1)
If these Monica Lewinskys don't put a smile on puff daddy's face nothing will. The shop stocks a reasonable selection of cigars (including 10 brands of Cubans) intriguingly stored behind glass with a 'smoking' humidifier.
✉ #01-K1 Tanglin Mall, 163 Tanglin Rd ☎ 6836 0811 🚌 7, 77, 106, 111, 123, 132, 174 ◷ 11am-11pm

Treknology Bikes 3
(4, D1) Bikes are cheaper than in many European and neighbouring Asian countries. Pick up a basic model for $450; a good mountain bike for $1500; or a titanium frame for $10,000.
✉ #01-02 Tanglin Pl, 91 Tanglin Rd ☎ 6732 7119 🚌 7, 77, 106, 111, 123, 132 ◷ Mon-Fri 11am-7.30pm

Crazy Captain Condom to the rescue!

BODY & HEALTH

Singapore is a great place to pamper yourself with reflexology, massage, facials and spas of all kinds.

Amrita Spa (3, H7)
Singapore's most extensive spa, for members and hotel guests only, boasts a fitness centre, whirlpools, bubble and plunge pools, and blissful beauty and deluxe massage treatments. A 3hr package costs around $300.
✉ **#06-01 Raffles City Convention Centre, 2 Stamford Rd** ☎ **6336 4477** Ⓜ **Raffles City** ⏰ **6am-10pm, treatments available 10am-8pm**

Aspapra (3, O4)
This nifty massage joint features a 60 air-jet Seawater Hydro massage bath ($45 for 20mins). If that doesn't get you limbered up the Body Glow all-over body scrub ($45 for 30mins) and manipulative Swedish massage ($74 for 45mins) will. Couple rooms are available.
✉ **L6 Amara Singapore Hotel, 165 Tanjong Pagar Rd** ☎ **6879 2688** Ⓜ **Tanjong Pagar** ⏰ **10am-10pm**

Eu Yan Sang (3, M4)
This revamped Chinese medical and health supplies hall lacks the dusty intrigue of more traditional haunts, but stock comes with English instructions and staff are willing to help.
✉ **269A South Bridge Rd** ☎ **6223 4363** Ⓜ **Raffles City** ⏰ **Mon-Sat 8.30am-6pm**

Frontier's Hairdressers (4, C10)
Frontier's new digs in a retro-meets-Zen pod have only served to enhance their reputation for a damn good haircut. Chill-out sounds, a nifty coffee bar, aerodynamic barber chairs and chic shears by Hikiri transform a shear and trim into a 'lifestyle choice'.
✉ **#01-12 Regency House, 123 Penang Rd** ☎ **6235 2565** Ⓜ **Somerset** ⏰ **Mon-Sat 11am-8pm, Sun noon-6pm**

Passion (4, B3)
If the humidity is playing hell with your hair and making your mascara run head to Passion, a groovy hair and make-up salon catering to celebrities and the stars. Costs for cuts are $60-220, make-up $250+. Bookings are essential.
✉ **#02-01/02 Palais Renaissance, 390 Orchard Road** ☎ **6733 5638** Ⓜ **Orchard** ⏰ **Mon-Fri 11am-8pm, Sat 10am-7pm**

Sabun Cabane (4, D1)
Kooky hairdressing salon/art gallery in a warehouse-cum-living-room featuring modernist furnishings, floor-to-ceiling mirrors, groovy lighting, jazz and glasses of red. Artworks are changed monthly, bad looks changed daily. Cuts are $40-90, highlights $140-200.
✉ **#03-22 Tanglin Mall, 163 Tanglin Rd** ☎ **6235 2910** 🚌 **7, 77, 106, 111, 123, 132, 174** ⏰ **10am-7pm**

Shiatsu School (3, H3)
A massage here will iron out the kinks, improve circulation, disperse toxins and generally improve the flow of energy within the body. Decor is simple but scrupulously clean – no shoes are allowed but clients keep their clothes on during the massage. Try the charcoal facial ($100 for 50mins). Massage is $80.
✉ **280 River Valley Rd** ☎ **6836 1231** 🚌 **139, 32** ⏰ **Mon-Fri 9.30am-9pm, Sat-Sun 9.30am-6pm**

Spa in the Village (2, F7) The treatments at this spa sound edible. Try the Liquorice Root Soup (spa bath), $30, or a Wafer (dry-brush session followed by a herb infused hot towel body wrap), $90.
✉ **34C Lorong Mambong, Holland Village** ☎ **6467 7219** 🚌 **77, 106, 174** ⏰ **Mon-Fri 10am-8.30pm, Sat-Sun 10am-6.30pm**

Traditional Body Charm (3, D6)
Have a traditional Indian massage or facial using natural Jurlique products, henna tattooing and 'eyebrow threading' in a slightly run-down but interesting old building in Little India.
✉ **#02-01, 37 Kerbau Rd, Little India** ☎ **6336 9411** 🚌 **65, 97, 103, 106** ⏰ **Mon-Fri 11am-8pm, Sat 10am-7pm**

places to eat

Hurl a pair of chopsticks in any direction in Singapore and chances are they'll land in something edible. Chomping, munching, slurping and crunching are national hobbies and with good reason – the best thing about Singapore is its food.

Price Ranges

Price ranges are based on what we think you are likely to spend per person for a one- to two-course meal and non-alcoholic drink.

$	under $10
$$	$20-35
$$$	$36-70
$$$$	over $70

You can find just about every kind of international cuisine in Singapore, but you're most likely to stumble across Chinese, Indian and Malay foods. Subtly flavoured Cantonese food is famous for its dim sum and won ton; in contrast Sichuan uses red peppers, garlic and ginger. Hokkien cuisine has yellow noodles and clear broths, while Singapore's signature dish is Hainanese chicken rice. Peranakan-style food, often called Nonya, combines Chinese ingredients with the sauces and spices of Malay cuisine, which itself is characterised by coconut-milk curries and satay. Indian cuisine features fiery curries and rice from the south and tandoori and breads from the north. Indian Muslim cuisine is known for biryani. Fusion cuisine combines (and sometimes confuses) Eastern and Western ingredients and cooking methods.

Chinese restaurants will usually offer green tea as a drink, elsewhere lime juice reigns. Local cafes typically sell tea and coffee with sweetened condensed milk. Tiger Beer is the local favourite. Good restaurants offer wine but the prices will easily double your bill.

Each ethnic group has its own food rules. As a general rule, copy your hosts and don't serve yourself first, don't leave your chopsticks standing upright in a rice bowl and use only your right hand when eating without implements. It's OK to ask for a fork.

If you're planning to eat anywhere other than a hawker stall it's

Business Dining

For good service, fine food and tasteful setting try the following: **Lei Garden** (p. 89), **Jiang Nan Chun** (pp. 81-2), **Mezza9** (p. 82), **Raffles Grill** (p. 79) or **La Voix** (p. 76).

Strike a deal over your meal.

wise to book a table. Weekend and brunch bookings can fill up days in advance. Upmarket restaurants include a service charge but elsewhere tipping is optional. All restaurants (except hawker stalls) are non-smoking.

A meal for $2, $20 or $200 will leave you equally satisfied. Even Singapore's swankiest restaurants often offer economical lunch deals.

CHINATOWN

Belachan (3, M4)   **$$**
Nonya
With minimalist decor this place is thankfully free of kitsch costumed mannequins in dusty Nonya costumes. Instead focus your attention on the prawn and papaya soup or Grandma's *itek manis*, duck simmered in ginger and black bean sauce.
✉ 10 Smith St ☎ 6221 9810 Ⓜ Outram Park
🕐 Tues-Sun 11.30am-3pm, 6.30-10.30pm ♿

Broth (3, N3)   **$$$**
European/Fusion
On Duxton Hill, Broth is a pleasant surprise in an area populated chiefly by dubious-looking mens bars. Friendly staff, a simple white interior and ceiling fans give this place a welcoming, informal feel. Try the rare tuna with wasabi, followed by a brown sugar meringue.
✉ 21 Duxton Hill
☎ 6323 3353
Ⓜ Tanjong Pagar
🕐 Mon-Fri noon-2pm, 6-10.30pm, Sat 6-10.30pm

Chinatown Complex (3, M3)   **$**
Hawker Stalls
Don your gumboots and savour the damp and sticky sights of the wet market before sitting yourself down to a feast of local faves. Finish up with a caffeine hit at the Angler gourmet coffee and tea stall (level 2).
✉ Smith St
Ⓜ Outram Park
🕐 10am-10pm ♿ Ⓥ

Chinatown Street Food (3, M4)   **$**
Hawker Stalls
Lined with hawker stalls selling everything from ping-pong-like rice balls in peanut soup, traditional sweet-and-salty *rojak* salad and noodles galore, you'll

---

Hawker Centres

Hawker stalls and food centres offer great food, a relaxed dress code, reasonable prices and scrupulous hygiene. (Look for the 'ABC' signs: The letters represent an annually awarded grading, based on excellence in cleanliness and food hygiene.) Hawker favourites include laksa, *roti prata* (crispy croissant-like pancakes dipped into curry), Haianese chicken rice, *char kway teow* (broad noodles fried with sweet soy sauce), Hokkien *mee* (yellow wheat noodles fried with seafood, eggs and meat), *popiah* (spring rolls), *nasi lemak* (rice boiled in coconut milk, served with small fried fish, chicken and peanuts), *char siew* rice (roast pork with rice) and *kaya* toast (toast with egg and coconut topping). To try these dishes head to one of these food stall areas:

- **Newton Food Centre** (Newton Circus; 3, B2) gets a good rap from locals and tourists alike and it's open 24hrs.
- **New Bugis St** (3, F7), the sanitised version of the old, grungy one, right in the middle of the bustling open market, has Malay, Indonesian, Thai and Chinese food.
- **Tekka Centre** (Serangoon Rd; 3, D6) is a bustling wet market with Indian-Muslim food stalls. Opposite is the **Little India Arcade**, where you'll find vegetarian, Muslim, Keralan and Sri Lankan food.
- **Lavender Food Centre** (Jalan Besar near Lavender St; 3, B9), is less touristed than Newton and also stays open until the early hours of the morning.
- **Chinatown Complex** (cnr Sago & Trengganu Sts; 3, M3), has some of Singapore's best Chinese food stalls on the 2nd floor.
- **Maxwell Rd Hawker Centre** (cnr South Bridge & Maxwell Rds; 3, M4), is a great spot to see the hawkers at work.
- **Satay Club** (Read St; 3, J4) whose vendors once plied their trade at the Padang, is now in Clarke Quay, in the evenings. At 40c a pop it's worth a try!
- **Geylang Serai Market** (5, A3), just near the Malay Cultural Village in Katong, offers delicious Malay delicacies.

find it hard to escape Smith St with an empty stomach. Ideally explored with a hungry band of fellow gourmet adventurers.
✉ **Smith St** Ⓜ **Outram Park** ⏱ **11am-11pm** ♿ **V**

Ci Yan Organic Vegetarian Health Food (3, M4) S
Vegetarian
The tiny wooden tables and chairs and the spiritual book selection give this place a schoolhouse vibe. Try an organic coffee or a set meal – they're 100% vegetarian and contain no garlic or onions – just what you need to detox after a night out on Mohamed Sultan Rd.
✉ **2 Smith St** ☎ **6225 9026** Ⓜ **Outram Park** ⏱ **noon-10pm** ♿ **V**

Gorka Grill (3, M4) SS
Nepalese
Venture beyond the blackened windows and tuck into something from the high country in simple ethnic surrounds. Try the *kwanti ko jhole*, a light peppery soup, before tucking into the *jheenga papita*, a prawn curry in a papaya boat.
✉ **21 Smith St** ☎ **6227 0806** Ⓜ **Outram Park** ⏱ **noon-2.30pm, 6.30pm-9pm** ♿

Kibbutz Café (3, L5) SS
Israeli
This is a friendly, simple cafe serving up Israeli favourites, such as pitta with hummus, crispy falafels, juicy stuffed cabbage rolls and yummy halvah ice cream. Vegetarians and dairy-free dieters welcome.
✉ **#01-04 Capital Square, 25 Church St**

Keeping Sharks Safe from Human Jaws

Shark fin soup is considered a delicacy in Chinese cuisine and the dish is especially popular at wedding banquets. This isn't great news for the sharks who are caught only to have their fins cut off, before they are thrown, still bleeding, back into the sea to die. Ecology organisations such as WildAid and IWMC have launched campaigns against shark consumption in Singapore, Hong Kong and Taiwan. In 2002 shock postcards were distributed depicting a young Chinese couple at a wedding banquet surrounded by dead and bleeding sharks.

☎ **6438 2221** Ⓜ **Raffles Place** ⏱ **Tues-Sat noon-3pm, 6-10pm** ♿ **V**

L'Aigle d'Or (3, N3) SSSS
French Contemporary
The plush environs, intimate atmosphere and big dollar signs all spell 'special announcement'. Start with the asparagus and black truffle soup, followed by the whole pigeon with sweet garlic cream. We suggest hiding the engagement ring in your loved one's hot lemon soufflé. The set lunch ($36, drinks not included) is reasonably priced.
✉ **83 Duxton Rd** ☎ **6227 7678** Ⓜ **Tanjong Pagar** ⏱ **noon-2pm, 7pm-10pm**

La Voix (3, M4) SSS
French
A rather theatrical blend of oranges and blacks, textured woods and glass are used to create a striking space with private nooks. Mainstays are the grilled duck with foie gras sauce and the baked snails; carnivores should head straight to the sumptuously meaty New Zealand

beef. In typical French fashion a separate bar aims to offer smokers a refuge.
✉ **1 Club St** ☎ **6220 6586** Ⓜ **Raffles Place** ⏱ **Mon-Fri noon-2.30pm, 7-10.30pm, Sat 7-10.30pm**

Mama Africa (3, L5) SSS
African
This is as far from dim sum as you will find in Singapore. Favourite choices here include crocodile with yellow rice, the grilled buffalo with a side serve of maize and the mixed African platter with *boerewors* (spicy sausages).
✉ **#01-01 Far East Square, 88 Telok Ayer St** ☎ **6532 9339** Ⓜ **Raffles Place** ⏱ **11.30am-2.30pm, 6.30-10.15pm** ♿

Nectar (3, M4) SSS
French Japanese
Nectar manages to be cosy and over-the-top all at once. When you see the 28-seat glowing alabaster marble centre table, the gold teardrop lights and gauzy gold-sheathed walls you'll understand why. Specialities include foie gras, soft crab in tangy

lime sauce, and teriyaki cod. The taste is succulent and the service attentive but if you're feeling hungry order plenty as the serves are small.

✉ 87 Club St ☎ 6323 4544 Ⓜ Raffles Place
🕐 Mon-Sat 11.30am-2.30pm, 6.30-10pm

Paolo E Judie
(3, N3) $$$
Italian
Hats off to designer Mok Wei Wei for the sleek brown-and-white minimalist interiors which make this place look a million dollars – which coincidentally is around how much it cost to create. Try Venice-born chef Paolo Scarpa's antipastos, black cuttlefish pasta or the codfish with rosemary. Unfortunately, the dishes don't quite live up to the deluxe surroundings.

✉ 81 Neil Rd
☎ 6225 8306
Ⓜ Tanjong Pagar
🕐 Mon-Fri 11am-2.30pm, 6.30-11.30pm, Sat 6.30-11.30pm

Qun Zhong Eating House (3, N3) $
Chinese Dumplings
Lunchtime queues extend out onto the street for the seafood, pork and vegetable dumplings cunningly rolled by a team of old ladies up the back of this red-and-white shophouse. A set of 8-10 dumplings, steamed or fried, go for

$7. Mmm...they're delicious *and* nutritious. Or try the Chinese pigeon ($9).

✉ 21 Neil Rd ☎ 6221 3060 Ⓜ Tanjong Pagar
🕐 11.30am-3pm, 5.30-9.30pm ♿ Ⓥ

Senso (3, M4) $$$
Italian
Senso's courtyard terrace is especially pleasant on balmy evenings when the well-heeled chow down over pan-fried duck's liver, fluffy, filling gnocchi and a cooling gelato to end. The attached modern/Jap fusion bar is rather pretentious but a favourite with the cigar set.

✉ 21 Club St
☎ 6224 3534
Ⓜ Raffles Place
🕐 Mon-Fri noon-2.30pm, 6-10.30pm, Sat-Sun 6-10.30pm

Shev Shev
(3, O3) $$$
Mediterranean
By now you've probably had enough Asiatic accented white-and-brown minimalist interiors to last a lifetime, but at least there's nothing to distract you from your food. Try the osso bucco or the baked eggplant and finish off with a drink downstairs at the bar.

✉ 66 Tanjong Pagar Rd
☎ 6224 0881
Ⓜ Tanjong Pagar
🕐 Mon-Fri 12pm-2pm, 7pm-11pm, Sat 7pm-11pm

Soup Restaurant
(3, M4) $$
Chinese Soup
Part of a small chain established by four women from Samsui, China, this cosy branch features traditional round wooden tables and cute little chairs. The specialities are the herbal double boiled soups with medicinal properties and Samsui ginger chicken to prevent coldness and cure 'windiness' in the body.

✉ 25 Smith St ☎ 6222 9923 Ⓜ Outram Park
🕐 noon-2pm, 6-9.30pm ♿ Ⓥ

Union (3, M4) $$$
Modern European Fusion
The stainless steel kitchen and polished wooden floors lend contemporary lines, but the wood lattice which climbs the walls and curves overhead, the egg chairs and jazz on the CD player give this place its trademark groove. Try the croquette de fromage or get an iron hit with a grilled prime sirloin steak. Economical set lunches are also on offer.

✉ 81 Club St ☎ 6327 4990 Ⓜ Raffles Place
🕐 noon-2.30pm, 6.30-10.30pm

Yum Cha Restaurant
(3, M4) $$
Yum Cha
This cavernous place serves from early till late so there's no excuse for going hungry. Nibble on bite-sized prawn and abalone dumplings at bite-sized prices, or stuff yourself stupid on fried Hong Kong noodles.

✉ #02-01, 20 Trengganu St ☎ 6372 1717 Ⓜ Outram Park
🕐 8am-11pm ♿ Ⓥ

Wildlife in Chinatown.

COLONIAL CENTRE

Christa & Naomi Café (CAN) (3, G8) $
Cafe

Crowded with mismatched furniture and second-hand treasures ranging from gas masks to musical instruments CAN Café is a delightful antidote to Singaporean order – and don't the kids love it! Twenty-somethings smoke cigarettes while downing beers or the house speciality – strawberry soda floaters. Music ranges from jazz to trance.

✉ #01-12/13/14, 1 Liang Seah St ☎ 6337 3732 Ⓜ Bugis ⏱ Sun-Thurs 3pm-1am, Fri-Sat 3pm-2am

Dome (3, G6) $$
Cafe

We're not mad about the franchise atmosphere but the location in a colonial building at the Singapore Art Museum is terrific. Mains are nothing to brag about but the coffee and cake ain't bad.

✉ Singapore Art Museum, 71 Bras Basah Rd ☎ 6339 0792 Ⓜ City Hall ⏱ 8.30am-10.30pm ♿

Dunhuang Tea House (3, G8) $$
Taiwanese Teahouse

Decked out like a whimsical vision of heaven in minimalist white with gauzy pastel-and-gold screens, this rickety Taiwanese teahouse aims to fill you with beauty and bring you to inner peace. Try a pot of jasmine tea with some famous pineapple biscuits or the kitsch Moonlight Meal, which sets the table aglow.

✉ 20 Liang Seah St

☎ 6837 2543 Ⓜ City Hall ⏱ 11am-10pm ♿ Ⓥ

Equinox, the Restaurant (3, H7) $$$
Eastern & Western

Superlatives just can't describe the jaw-dropping view from this 70th-floor restaurant in IM Pei's Swissôtel (he's the guy responsible for the Louvre's glass pyramid in Paris). Soaring ceilings, Asiatic wall hangings and plush fabrics only enhance the surrounds. It's unlikely the quality of your meal will quite measure up to the view but at least with pure East and West there's no con-Fusion. The similar New Asia Bar & Grill (p. 94) is next door.

✉ L70, Swissôtel, 2 Stamford Rd ☎ 6837 3322 Ⓜ City Hall ⏱ noon-2.30pm, 7-11pm

Imperial Herbal Restaurant (3, G7) $$
Chinese Health Food

Above the Metropole Hotel the in-house Chinese physician can check your pulse and tongue and prescribe something on the menu that will get your yin and yang back in balance. Whether you're after an aphrodisiac, want to improve your complexion or stop your hair greying prematurely, there is a herbal soup or some other dish for you.

✉ Metropole Hotel, 41 Seah St ☎ 6337 0491 Ⓜ City Hall ⏱ 11.30am-2.30pm, 6.30-10.30pm ♿ Ⓥ

Jaan (3, H7) $$$
French

Compared to Equinox's flamboyance Jaan's wood panelling and simple olive and maroon tones are positively minimalist. However the Murano glass 'chandelier' that spans the length of the ceiling like a trio of sea serpents gives the game away. At Jaan (which means 'bowl' in Sanskrit) you can sample Khmer-influenced French fare by an Italian chef fresh from Spoons in London: multiculturalism gone mad.

✉ L70, Swissôtel, 2 Stamford Rd ☎ 6837 3322 Ⓜ City Hall ⏱ noon-2.30pm, 7-11pm

La Fete de Cuisinier (3, F6) $$$
Creole

Decked out in antiques and featuring a lovely courtyard, Singapore's only French Creole restaurant serves up New Orleans fare in grand surrounds. With a no mobile phone policy and a teensy seven-table dining room romance is almost guaranteed. Reservations and tasteful attire are essential.

✉ 161 Middle Rd ☎ 6333 0917 Ⓜ Bugis ⏱ noon-2pm, 7-10.30pm

Lighthouse (3, K7) $$$$
European

Perched atop the Fullerton Hotel the tiny Lighthouse restaurant boasts a fabulous view onto the marina including a bird's-eye view of the Esplanade. However the intimate atmosphere can be marred somewhat by a stream of hotel guests and

Singapore Sling

Singapore's famous cocktail was created at Raffles Hotel in 1915 by a Hainanese Chinese bartender called Ngiam Tong Boon. Raffles' Bar & Billiard Room is still making a killing serving up this cocktail to tourists, however, they do let you throw peanut shells on the floor, which is a saving of almost $1000 in littering fines. The record for excessive Singapore slinging is held by five Australians who consumed 131 Singapore Slings in two hours in 1985.

tourists coming up for an eyeful. There's an extensive wine list and the dining is accomplished.
✉ **Fullerton Hotel, 1 Fullerton Sq ☎ 6877 8932 Ⓜ Raffles Place** ⏰ noon-2.30pm, 7-10pm

Marmalade
(3, G7) $$$
European Fusion
Minimalist design in textured chocolate and creamy tones, soothing French House tunes and flavoursome if nouvelle-sized meals of an Asiatic-cum-Mediterranean ilk make Marmalade one of Singapore's coolest hangs. If you're still hungry try nibbling on one of the tasty-looking staff.
✉ **36 Purvis St ☎ 6837 2123 Ⓜ City Hall** ⏰ Mon-Fri 6.30pm-midnight, Fri-Sat 6.30pm-1am

Paladino (3, G6) $$$
Italian
Small but sumptuous, the Paladino is decked in golds and chocolates like a 1930s luxury ocean liner dining room. Intimate atmosphere, Fendi-inspired furnishings and a modern take on north Italian cuisine make for a singular experience. It also offers

afternoon tea and a reasonably priced set lunch.
✉ **Singapore Art Museum, 71 Bras Basah Rd ☎ 6738 0917 Ⓜ City Hall** ⏰ Tues-Sun lunch 11am-3pm, tea 3-6pm, dinner 6-10pm

Raffles (3, H7) $-$$$$
Asian & European
Raffles Hotel has a host of fine eateries, ranging from its budget and child-friendly bakery with dim sum, to the 'trans-ethnic' cuisine and curtained cubicles of **Doc Cheng's**, the Chinese Inn ambience of the **Empress Room** and the colonial **Long Bar Steakhouse** specialising in plantation cuisines such as jumbo skewers and tamarind and sugar-cane-flavoured short ribs. The **Billiard Room** is ideal for brunch. Reservations for restaurants are essential.
✉ **Raffles Hotel, 1 Beach Rd ☎ 6337 1886 Ⓜ City Hall** ⏰ noon-2pm, 7-10pm

Rossi Restaurant
(3, G7) $$
Italian
The bar downstairs is a little stark and uninviting but upstairs cream walls and murals create a surprisingly cosy atmosphere. Try the pumpkin tortellini with

sage or the linguine with white wine and clams. Note the later than usual opening hours.
✉ **7 Purvis St ☎ 6333 0147 Ⓜ City Hall** ⏰ Mon-Fri noon-2.30pm, Mon-Thur 6.30pm-midnight, Fri-Sat 6.30pm-1am

Sakana (3, G8) $$
Japanese
This is a super-cute, unpretentious Japanese restaurant featuring tiny screened booths and a range of sake. Try the set lunch for $19.
✉ **#01-03/04 Liang Seah St ☎ 6336 0266 Ⓜ Bugis** ⏰ 11.30am-2.30pm, 6-10.30pm

Victorian Café
(3, K6) $
Cafe
This pint-sized caff with old-fashioned marble-topped tables and modest chandeliers sells fairly average but modestly priced sandwiches, hotdogs and Asian specials – which are probably the pick of the bunch. It's ideal for a rest stop or pre-concert drink.
✉ **Victoria Concert Hall, 11 Empress Place ☎ 6338 4083 Ⓜ Raffles Place** ⏰ 11.30am-3pm, 6-10pm (concert nights only) ♿

Yakitori Restaurant
(3, G8) $
Japanese
Casual, open-air corner eatery – pick up Japanese to go or stay and chew the fat for a while.
✉ **516 North Bridge Rd ☎ 6338 8473 Ⓜ Bugis** ⏰ noon-2.30pm, 6-10.30pm ♿

ORCHARD ROAD

If you're a fan of shopping malls, big hotel chains, cheesy restaurant franchises and overpriced coffee you'll be in gastronomic heaven along Orchard Rd – go crazy! If not, give these a try. If you're starving and want to eat for a few dollars head to a shopping mall food court – you'll find them at basement level.

Blu (4, A1)   **$$$$**
Fusion
By night Blu glows its namesake colour and diners enjoy a great view and international jazz performers. Start with Iranian caviar or the famous crab and pistachio bisque before tackling the grilled US prime beef or oven-baked ratatouille. Reservations are essential. Wines range from $60 to $3000 (ay carumba!).
✉ **24th fl, Shangri-La Hotel, 22 Orange Grove Rd** ☎ **6730 2598** Ⓜ **Orchard** ⏰ **Mon-Sat 7-10.30pm** Ⓥ

Bombay Woodlands Restaurant (4, C2) **$$**
Indian Vegetarian
With dowdy decor but impeccable ethics, the dears here state that violence breeds violence and that if we stopped killing animals maybe we'd stop killing each other. They also do a reasonably priced set lunch.
✉ **#B1-01/02 Tanglin Shopping Centre, 19 Tanglin Rd** ☎ **6235 2712** 🚌 **7, 77, 106, 111, 123, 132, 174** ⏰ **9.30am-10pm** ⚤ Ⓥ

Chatterbox (4, C7) **$$**
East & West
It's ugly and full of tourists but Chatterbox is open 24hrs and is one of the best places to try Singapore's famous Hainanese chicken rice. Help yourself to tender

chicken, unlimited servings of fragrant, fluffy rice and condiments of dark soy, chilli and freshly ground ginger.
✉ **South Tower Lobby, Mandarin Singapore, 333 Orchard Rd** ☎ **6831 6291** Ⓜ Somerset ⏰ **24hrs** ⚤

Cuppage Terrace (4, B9)   **$$-$$$**
Mixed
Just off Orchard Rd you'll find a number of shophouse restaurants with outdoor tables at Cuppage Terrace. The touting here can be aggressive and you won't find much in the way of fine dining but it's a pleasant spot for a beer.
✉ **Cuppage Rd** Ⓜ **Somerset** ⏰ **approx noon-2.30pm, 6.30-10pm**

DKNY Café (4, B3) **$**
Cafe
What the hell are you doing in a DKNY café? Get your fashion victim credentials stamped over coffee ($4) and bagels ($3-7)

while leafing through some mags – or make believe you're an undercover agent for the fashion police and take polaroids of all the badly dressed shoppers passing by.
✉ **#01-03 Palais Renaissance, 390 Orchard Rd** ☎ **6734 0811** Ⓜ **Orchard** ⏰ **Mon-Sat 11am-7pm, Sun 11.30am-5.30pm**

Esmirada (4, C8)   **$$**
Mediterranean
Choose from reasonably priced couscous, paella, moussaka, lasagne and bouillabaisse in a faux hacienda ambience. Nonetheless it's one of the most tasteful spots for refuelling on this strip.
✉ **Peranakan Place, 180 Orchard Rd** ☎ **6735 3476** Ⓜ **Somerset** ⏰ **noon-2.30pm, 6-10pm** ⚤

Graffiti Café (4, C7)   **$**
Cafe
In graffiti-free Singapore it's easy to see why this place

Great Views
For bird's-eye views of Singapore consider **Blu**, **Equinox** (p. 78), **Top of the M** (p. 82) or **Lighthouse** (p. 78-9). For waterfront breezes try **Siem Reap II** (p. 87) or **Indochine Waterfront** (p. 86) at Empress Place, **Pierside** (p. 87), **Harry's Bar** (p. 99) or other recommended restaurants on Boat Quay. For greenery try **Au Jardin Les Amis** (p. 88) or **Halia** (p. 89) at the Botanic Gardens.

is popular with schoolkids. Jammed between micro fashion boutiques and the video game parlour the Graffiti Café serves up bubble milk tea and cheap curry dinners. You can put your own doodles up on the walls alongside some sophisticated manga-style offerings without worrying about getting beaten around with the rotan later on.
✉ **#04-24/26 The Heeren, 260 Orchard Rd**
☎ 6738 0424
Ⓜ Somerset
🕐 10am-10pm ♿

Grounds (4, C4) **$$**
Japanese Cafe
This small white restaurant features cosy booths, gauzy fuchsia screens and park views. Drop in for coffee,

Hui Cui cuisine; for lovers of Cantonese.

wine or sake, Japanese tapas or the set lunch. Dare yourself to eat the weird-looking Kyoto seafood pizza. Serves are on the small side.
✉ **L2, Wheelock Pl, 501 Orchard Rd** ☎ **6820 3301** Ⓜ Orchard
🕐 Mon-Fri 11.30am-10.30pm, Sat-Sun 11.30am-midnight

House of Mao Hunan Hot Pot (4, B2) **$$**
Hunanese
This place provides a DIY

buffet and hot pot surrounded by Mao memorabilia in a hard-to-find franchise atmosphere. More fun than the Cultural Revolution! Try the herbal jelly with quintang. Child serves are available.
✉ **#01-09/10 Orchard Hotel Shopping Arcade, 442 Orchard Rd**
☎ 6733 7667
Ⓜ Orchard
🕐 11.30am-3pm, 6-10.30pm ♿ **V**

Hu Cui (4, C6) **$$$**
Cantonese
Follow the green glass tunnel into a shadowy room of earthy browns and greys that make it easy to forget you're in a shopping mall and eating in a fashionably branded branch of the popular Crystal Jade chain. If you don't feel like paying for decor try the relaxed, family-friendly Crystal Jade in the Shaw Centre (4, B2).
✉ **#02-12 Ngee Ann City, 391 Orchard Rd**
☎ 6238 1011 Ⓜ Orchard 🚌 7, 65, 106, 124, 167, 174 🕐 11.30am-3pm, 6-11pm

Jiang Nan Chun (4, C3) **$$$**
Cantonese
The dark wood, starkly contrasting lighting and impeccable service make for a slightly intense atmosphere, but this stylish restaurant with sophisticated menu is ideal for impressing

Brunch and High Tea
Modern Singapore has inherited the Brits' mania for elaborate buffet brunches and toffy-style high teas. The best spot for both are five-star hotels that lay out Eastern and Western savouries, cakes, puddings, fruits and even champagne for the hungry hordes. Prices range from $45-80 per head, young kids sometimes eat for free and child-minding facilities may be available. To be assured of a seat book several days ahead. Try **Mezza9** at the Grand Hyatt (p. 82; ☎ 6730 7188), the charming waterfall room at **Sheraton Towers** (☎ 6737 6888), Raffles' colonial-style **Bar & Billiard Room** (p. 79; ☎ 6331 1612), **One-Ninety** at the Four Seasons Hotel (☎ 6831 7250) or the waterfront **Post** at the Fullerton (p. 95; ☎ 6733 8388).

Caffeine Boost

Despite its narcotic-style kick and addictive qualities coffee is not illegal in Singapore. Avoid the bland international franchises and head to a traditional coffee house where an iced black coffee or hot cuppa sweetened with condensed milk is just what you need to feel full of beans.

The taking of tea in Singapore can be a refined ritual. Arguably the best-known teahouse is **Tea Chapter** (9A Neil Rd; 3, M4; ☎ 6226 1175; open 11am-11pm), where Queen Elizabeth and hubby Prince Philip drank tea in 1989, here you can learn about the art of tea drinking and purchase Asian and herbal teas to take away. Nearby the **Yixing Yuan Teahouse** (30 Tanjong Pagar Rd; 3, N4; ☎ 6224 6961; open 11am-11pm) offers the same thing.

business colleagues. Try the deep-fried crispy eel or crab claws in marinade. Private rooms are available by reservation.

✉ **Four Seasons Hotel, 190 Orchard Blvd**
☎ 6734 1110 Ⓜ Orchard ◷ 11.30am-2.30pm, 6-10.30pm

Mezza9 (4, B5) $$-$$$
Asian

Housing a number of concepts under one roof, this cavernous, market-type food area at the Hyatt is popular with business people and offers a good range of Asian cuisines at reasonable prices, but it's hard to forget you're in a hotel lobby.

✉ **Grand Hyatt Hotel, 10/12 Scotts Rd**
☎ 6730 7188/9
Ⓜ Orchard
◷ noon-2.30pm, 6.30-10.30pm V

Nooch (4, C4) $$
Noodles

This streamlined timber and stainless steel Asian noodle bar has views onto the park and hip-looking waiters giving orders by headphone

sets. Try the *kamon udon* with smoked duck and mountain vegetables and the thirst-quenching *momo* fruit cocktail.

✉ **#02-16 Wheelock Pl, 501 Orchard Rd**
☎ 6235 0880
Ⓜ Orchard ◷ Sun-Thur 11.30am-2pm, 6-10pm, Fri-Sat 11.30am-10.30pm V

Royal Copenhagen Tea Lounge (4, C6) $$
Tea Room

A fierce contender in the Tokyo 2002 International Competition for Most Uptight Restaurant Names, this department-store tea room does serve an elegant pot in their namesake posh porcelain. The menu suggests you 'Enjoy a conversational afternoon with friends by nibbling sweets and sipping tea'...delightful. Boasts a bird's-eye view onto Orchard Rd's shopper ants.

✉ **L2, Takashimaya Ngee Ann City, 391A Orchard Rd**
☎ 6735 6833
Ⓜ Somerset, Orchard
🚌 7, 65, 106, 124, 167, 174 ◷ 10am-9pm ♿

Top of the M
(4, C7) $$$$
Continental

See the whole of Singapore without moving an inch from this 39th-floor revolving restaurant. Specialities include the lobster bisque and crepes suzette but we recommend booking ahead for the prime rib of beef.

✉ **39th fl, Mandarin Singapore, 333 Orchard Rd** ☎ 6831 6258
Ⓜ Orchard ◷ noon-2.30pm, 6.30-10.30pm

See? There are quiet cafes in Singapore.

ORCHARD ROAD AREA

Armenian Kopitiam
(3, H5)   **$**
Hawker Cafe
Directly across from the
Armenian branch of the
Asian Civilisations
Museum this typical cafe is
ideal for *char kway teow,
nasi padang* and kick-ass
Chinese coffee. Flip-flops
and T-shirts are de rigueur.
✉ **34 Armenian St**
☎ **6339 6575**
Ⓜ **City Hall**
🕐 **7am-9pm** ♿

Domus (3, B1)   **$$$**
Italian
This upmarket Italian
eatery offers impeccable
service and refined sur-
rounds. Signature dishes
include home-made tagli-
atelle with porcini mush-
rooms, asparagus and
black truffles in white wine
and old-fashioned home-
style dishes like oven-
baked rack of lamb with
seasonal vegetables and
rosemary. There is an
Italian wine list.
Reservations are essential.
✉ **Sheraton Towers,
39 Scotts Rd** ☎ **6839
5622** Ⓜ **Newton**
🕐 **6.30-10.30pm** **V**

Fat Frog Café
(3, H5)   **$$**
Cafe
This funky cafe attached to
Substation arts centre pro-
vides Singapore's alternative
crowd with a haunt. Snack
and sip in the large court-
yard which doubles as a
rock stage on weekends.
✉ **45 Armenian St**
☎ **6338 6201**
Ⓜ **City Hall** 🚌 **97,
124, 167** 🕐 **Sun-Thur
11.30am-11pm, Fri-Sat
11.30am-1am** ♿

Gordon Grill
(3, C1)   **$$$**
Continental
Decorated with lashings of
pinkish beige, the
Goodwood Park Hotel is
hard to love for its looks.
Carnivores won't mind. Sink
those teeth into marble-fat
Kobe beef – hand reared,
milk fed and sold by 100g
weight for your dining
pleasure.
✉ **Goodwood Park
Hotel, 22 Scotts Rd**
☎ **6730 1744**
Ⓜ **Orchard** 🕐 **noon-
2.30am, 7-10.30pm**

Killiney Kopitiam
(4, D9)   **$**
Cafe
The waiter yells your order
at ear-splitting volume and
the coffee – shaken by the
resulting seismic disturbance
– inevitably arrives erupted
into the saucer. But this
popular cafe is *the* place to
breakfast on 'KOPI!!' and
'KAYA TOOOOASSST!!!!'.
✉ **67 Killiney Rd**
☎ **6734 3910**
Ⓜ **Somerset** 🕐 **Mon,
Wed-Sat 6am-11pm,
Tues & Sun 6am-6pm** ♿

Li Bai (3, B1)   **$$$**
Modern Cantonese
This is one of Singapore's
best and most popular swish
Chinese restaurants, situated
in the basement of Sheraton
Towers. Dine amid red-lit
banners with jade-coloured
chopsticks. Specials may
include 'Mini Buddha Jumps
Over The Wall' or barbecue
suckling pig. Reservations
are recommended.
✉ **Sheraton Towers,
39 Scotts Rd** ☎ **6839
5623** Ⓜ **Newton**
🕐 **lunch noon-2pm,
dinner 6.30-10.30pm** **V**

Rice Roll & Porridge
(4, D9)   **$**
Chinese
This simple eatery is reputed
to have the best congee in
town, but don't forget to
try a deliciously squidgy
savoury rice roll floating in
soy sauce, or its speciality
– sweet rolls stuffed with
yam, mango and durian
fillings.
✉ **69 Killiney Rd**
☎ **6736 1355**
Ⓜ **Somerset**
🕐 **Mon-Fri 9am-11pm**
♿ **V**

Spoiled for choice, lah!

LITTLE INDIA & ARAB STREET

Andhra Curry
(3, D6)   **$$**
Indian
If you've had enough of Indian hawker stalls try this this simple, pleasant restaurant. It specialises in the fiery food characteristic of the Indian state of Andhra Pradesh – don't miss the Andhra Hyderabadi *biryani* or *kalyana bhojana*, the traditional vegetarian wedding dish.
✉ **41 Kerbau Rd**
☎ **6293 3935** 🚌 **65, 97, 103, 106** ⏱ **noon-2.30pm, 6-10pm** ♿ **V**

Bangles (3, E8)   **$$**
Indian
Housed in a cosy pre-war shophouse decorated with Indian furniture, carpets and brassware, this 26-seat restaurant specialises in North Indian and Mughlai cuisine and also offers a reasonable range of vegetarian dishes. Try the tandoori, the chicken cashew masala or a scrumptious crayfish curry. Desserts include the lip-smacking *falooda*, a sweet, rose-flavoured milky drink.
✉ **5 Jalan Kledek**
☎ **6295 1755** Ⓜ **Bugis** ⏱ **11am-2pm, 6-10pm** ♿ **V**

Bumbu (3, E9)   **$$**
Indonesian
This delightful restaurant near the Sultan Mosque features an elegant upstairs dining room complete with traditional furnishings and a giant antique gramophone. Try the stuffed squid in lime sauce or the special prawn and century egg Bumbu salad. Finish up with gooey glutinous rice and durian for dessert.
✉ **44 Kandahar St**

☎ **6392 8628** Ⓜ **Bugis** ⏱ **11am-2pm, 6-10pm** ♿

Café Le Caire
(3, F9)   **$$**
Middle Eastern
The only problem with this Egyptian stall is once you start eating here it requires an iron will to drag yourself away. Try its famous spring chicken in yoghurt and olive oil, the tremendously sweet and sticky *harissa*, or the lamb and okra stew. Leave space for coffee and pastries. By night the old guys come out with their water pipes to gossip.
✉ **39 Arab St** ☎ **6292 0979** Ⓜ **Bugis** ⏱ **9am-9pm** ♿

French Stall
(3, A8)   **$$**
French
Owned and run by a two-star Michelin chef from Brittany, the French Stall in the heart of Little India is like any other Singaporean hawker restaurant except the food is French, the wine is good and about half the clientele have EEC passports. The three-course set meal is a good deal, otherwise sample the mussels with aioli sauce, the pork with ratatouille or the beef fondue. Miam! Note: it's cash only.
✉ **544 Serangoon Rd**
☎ **6299 3544** 🚌 **65, 97, 103, 106** ⏱ **Tues-Sun 6.30-10.30pm** ♿

Herbal Jelly Specialist
(3, F7)   **$-$$$$**
Herbal Jellies
It's not exactly lunch, but these herbal jellies aim to fulfil a variety of medicinal functions, such as curing 'heatiness' and improving your complexion. This is a popular haunt with age-conscious Chinese dames. Try the purifying logan jelly which promotes brain development and healthy *qi*.
✉ **#01-01, 52 Queen St** Ⓜ **Bugis** ⏱ **10am-late**

Komala Vilas
(3, D6)   **$**
Indian Vegetarian
The wildly popular Komala Vilas serves up terrific, cheap vegetarian meals all day long. You can snack on *samosas* (spicy stuffed pastries) or *bonda* (deep-fried potato) but the real drawing card is the *thali* – a host of vegetable curries, dhal and condiments, served on a banana leaf, that you eat with your right hand. Two doors down, Komala Vilas

Behind Little India's colourful shopfronts…

Sweet Shop serves take-away milky Indian sweets in edible foil wrappers.

✉ 76/78 Serangoon Rd
☎ 6293 6990
🚌 65, 97, 103, 106 ⏲ 7am-11pm ♿ V

Natural Café (3, E6) $
Chinese Health Cafe
A friendly couple serve up oil-, salt- and MSG-free mainly vegetarian fare in what used to be the heart of Singapore's backpackers district. A fish soup or *mee goreng* goes for around $4.

✉ #01-05 Burlington Sq, 175 Bencoolen St
☎ 6333 9770 🚌 64, 106, 111 ⏲ Mon-Sat 10am-8pm ♿ V

New Generation Vegetarian Eating House (3, C7) $
Vegetarian Chinese
This is a friendly, unpretentious open-air vegetarian cafe with specials. Try the mock duck or pineapple rice for $3.

✉ #01-01, 5 Hindoo Rd
☎ 6398 0878
🚌 65, 97, 103, 106
⏲ 8am-9pm ♿ V

Sabar Menanti (3, E9) $
Padang/Malay
This small shophouse with shady outdoor verandah really packs in the lunchtime crowd with its terrific Malay fare. Pick through platters piled high with tempting goodies, from fried chicken and curried eggs to bitter gourd and tender aubergine.

✉ 50/52 Kandahar St
☎ 6293 0284 Ⓜ Bugis
⏲ Mon-Sat 8am-8pm, Sun 8am-5pm ♿ V

Samlor (3, D6) $
Cafe
This shady 24hr cafe serves the usual condensed-milk tea and coffees, *roti prata*, Indian doughnuts and *nasi goreng* at the quiet end of Campbell St in the hub of Little India. This is a great spot to write postcards, soak up the local vibe and feel smugly superior to the odd red-faced, camera-laden tourist group passing by.

✉ 68 Campbell La
🚌 65, 97, 103, 106
⏲ 24hrs ♿

Si Chuan Dou Hua Seafood Restaurant (3, F8) $$$
Sichuan
We're not overly fond of hotel restaurants, but this one has a good reputation for feisty Sichuan flavours in reasonably tasteful surrounds – rare around this strip. Try the double-boiled bamboo pith soup, followed by camphor tea smoked duck. A cooling jelly and ice cream for dessert will displace any 'heatiness'. Chinese wines could be a novelty.

✉ Plaza Hotel, 7500A Beach Rd ☎ 6298 0011 Ⓜ Bugis
⏲ noon-2.30pm, 7-10pm

Wing Seong Fatty's (Albert) Restaurant (3, E6) $$
Chinese
Fatty's has been a favourite with Westerners since British troops were stationed in Singapore during WWII. Today it serves up cheap, enormous portions to locals and Singapore's backpacker population all at lightning speed.

✉ #01-31 Burlington Sq, 175 Bencoolen St
☎ 6338 1087 🚌 64, 106, 111 ⏲ noon-11pm

Zam Zam (3, E8) $
Indian
These guys have been churning out the goods since 1900 so we figure they probably know what they're doing. Watch those clever *murtabak* makers at work before hoeing into a mutton-, chicken- or vegetable-filled one of your own.

✉ 699 North Bridge Rd
☎ 6298 7011 Ⓜ Bugis
⏲ 7am-11pm ♿ V

...lurks some of the spiciest food in Singapore.

THE QUAYS

Bastiani (3, J4) $$$$
Mediterranean
This upmarket, slightly uptight waterside eatery offers specialities like its prize-winning lobster bisque and delectable combinations like lamb with wild rice risotto, braised figs and grilled leeks in a rosemary sauce. Expect grown-up dining with prices to match.
✉ #01-12, 3A Clarke Quay Rd ☎ 6433 0156 🚌 65, 139, 970 🕐 noon-2.30pm

Coriander Leaf (3, J2) $$$
Fusion
So, there's no riverside view and the decor makes it hard to forget you're in a hotel restaurant, but man oh man is the food fine! The sea bass with tomatoes, coriander rice and spicy marmalade is really something special while the Brazilian hot chocolate pudding is positively evil.
✉ #02-01 Gallery Hotel, 76 Robertson Quay ☎ 6732 3354 🚌 65, 139, 970 🕐 Mon-Fri noon-2pm, 6.30-10pm, Sat 6.30-10.30pm

En (3, H3) $$
Japanese
This casual Japanese dining bar has modernist aspirations but falls short with a Flintstones vibe. Enjoy standard Jap fare, sake and beer before a night clubbing on Mohamed Sultan Rd.
✉ #01-57, 207 River Valley Rd ☎ 6735 2212 🚌 65, 139, 970 🕐 noon-2.30pm, 6pm-late

Hot Stones (3, L6) $$
Seafood
One of the more tasteful if bemusing options along this otherwise garish strip, Hot Stones features a giant replica dinosaur skeleton upstairs. Extinct-guish (sorry!) your appetite with a plate of sauteed NZ mussels or evolve your palate to a salmon fillet.
✉ 53 Boat Quay ☎ 6534 5188 🚇 Raffles Place 🕐 noon-2.30pm, 6-10.30pm ⚓

Indochine Waterfront (3, K6) $$$
South-East Asian
This upmarket branch enjoys enviable views, balmy evening breezes and sublime surrounds. Director Michael Ma recently flew 300 partygoers to Germany to celebrate the opening of Indochine's Hamburg branch. You'll find echoes of this flamboyance in Indochine's calculated poshness – check out the giant chandeliers. Otherwise the menu is a slightly more sophisticated and expensive version of the usual Vietnamese, Cambodian and Laotian inspired dishes.
✉ Asian Civilisations Museum, 1 Empress Place ☎ 6339 1720 🚇 Raffles Place 🕐 noon-2.30pm, 7pm-late Ⓥ

Kinara (3, L6) $$
Punjabi
One of the best picks along Boat Quay, you can dine riverside or inside the renovated shophouse which is outfitted to look like a *haveli* (a traditional, ornately decorated Indian residence). It can be noisy around here.
✉ 57 Boat Quay ☎ 6533 0412 🚇 Raffles Place 🕐 11.30am-2.30pm, 6.30-10.30pm ⚓

The Food Detective

Wrapped in a trench coat and cunningly disguised by dark glasses, Makansutra, flamboyant TV food detective, tracks down hawker stalls and food centres far and wide in search of Singapore's best and brightest. You can pick up a copy of the Makansutra definitive hawker food guide at good bookshops (see p. 70-1) or check out 🄴 www.makansutra .com for the latest reviews and food tours.

La Brasserie (3, K4) $$$
Contemporary Chinese
The soft creams and golds and special-occasion ambience make for grown-up fine dining. Try a Peking duck crepe, followed by the rather intriguing baked pork ribs with mocha sauce. The hot almond cream could well be the dish to send you over the edge. Afterwards head downstairs to Le Bar (p. 94) for a boogie.
✉ Asian Restaurant and Bar, 50 Eu Tong Sen St ☎ 6532 6006 🚌 63, 124, 174, 197 🕐 12.30-2.30pm, 6.30-10.30pm

Le Restaurant
(3, K4) $$$
South-East Asian & Japanese
Set in a recently revamped 120-year-old Chinese building (the former Tong Chai Medical Institute), Le Restaurant makes the most of its setting. Chic waitresses in little black dresses escort you via a bridge-cum-catwalk to your candle-lit courtyard table or to the lush opium-den-style indoors. The food is good but not nearly as sexy as the surroundings. Try the lunchtime dim sum.
✉ **Asian Restaurant and Bar, 50 Eu Tong Sen St** ☎ **6532 6006** 🚌 **63, 124, 174, 197** ⏱ **12.30-2.30pm, 6.30-10.30pm**

Pierside (3, K7) $$$
Seafood
Owned by the Marmalade restaurant gang, Pierside's minimalist interiors, mirrored walls and alfresco dining give this spot the Singapore stamp of cool. Crunch and 'yum' your way through our fishy friends, from sea bass ceviche, cumin-spiced crab cakes and squid ink risotto to the signature 48hr-miso-marinated oven-baked cod. Mmm...
✉ **#01-01 One Fullerton, 1 Fullerton Rd** ☎ **6438 0400** 🚇 **Raffles Place** ⏱ **noon-2.30pm, 7-10.30pm**

Restaurant Kei
(3, J2) $$$
Japanese
In the industrial-hip Gallery Hotel this restaurant boasts Japanese with a Euro twist. Cast tradition aside and try its signature foie gras sushi, followed by grilled mackerel in sea salt and dessert of green tea ice cream. Head

downstairs to the Sound Bar (p. 95) for a riverside beer to follow.
✉ **#01-10 Gallery Hotel, 76 Robertson Quay** ☎ **6738 1551** 🚌 **65, 139, 970** ⏱ **noon-2.30pm, 7-10pm**

Siem Reap II
(3, K6) $$
South-East Asian
The menu is similar to Indochine Waterfront (p. 86) next door. The waterfront setting is especially lovely by night, while Asian antiques and chilling electronica make for a hip, modern Asia ambience. The staff are cute to look at but service is a tad flaky – groups may find individual orders arriving staccato style.
✉ **Asian Civilisations Museum, 1 Empress Place** ☎ **6338 7596** 🚇 **Raffles Place** ⏱ **meals: 11am-2.30pm, 6.30pm-11pm, drinks: 11am-midnight** ♿ **V**

Sultan 8 (3, H3) $
Cafe
Feeling a bit boozy and bleary-eyed? Perhaps it's time for a carbo-hit at this late-night eatery before venturing back to the clubs along Mohamed Sultan Rd. Have eggs on toast or a hearty *mee goreng* with a Red Bull on the side.
✉ **8 Mohamed Sultan**

Rd ☎ **6737 5181** 🚌 **65, 139, 970** ⏱ **Mon-Wed 10am-3am, Thur-Sat 10am-6am** **V**

Sundanese Food
(3, L6) $$
Indonesian
Low-key and friendly compared to the aggressive touters on Boat Quay, you can dine outside or upstairs in ethnic surrounds. Tickle your tonsils with a dancing fish or spicy Sudanese chicken washed down with cooling lime juice.
✉ **55/55A Boat Quay** ☎ **6534 3775** 🚇 **Raffles Place** ⏱ **Mon-Fri 11am-2.30pm, 6-10pm, Sat-Sun 6-10pm** ♿

Superbowl – the Art of Eating Congee
(3, L6) $$
Chinese
This superbly named restaurant offers dozens of MSG-free variations on the congee (Chinese porridge) theme – try it with seafood, meat, poultry, preserved eggs or go crazy with your own combination. Chow down riverside or enter via the Malay-inspired saloon doors and dine in cute 1940s-style booths.
✉ **80/80A Boat Quay** ☎ **6538 606** 🚇 **Raffles Place** ⏱ **11am-3pm, 6-11pm** ♿

Vegetarian Dining
Most fine restaurants offer a vegetarian option or two – call first to inquire. Otherwise, **Little India** (pp. 84-5) is packed with vegetarian curry joints and you'll find Chinese vegetarian in **Chinatown** (pp. 75-7) and the **East Coast** (p. 90). For fantastic vegetarian food and great service in fine surrounds taxi across town to **Original Sin** (p. 89) in Holland Village.

CHIJMES, BOTANIC GARDENS & BEYOND

Alkaff Mansion
(2, G8)   **$$$**
International
Set in a 1920s mansion built for a wealthy Dutch family, this is an elegant spot to try the Dutch-Indonesian *rijstaffel* (rice table of at least 10 dishes) served up by women in traditional Malay dress. You can also enjoy high tea, held on weekends from 3-5.30pm ($15).
✉ **10 Telok Blangah Green, Telok Blangah Hill Park (off Henderson Rd)** ☎ **6278 6979** ⏱ noon-2.30pm, 7-10.30pm

Au Jardin Les Amis
(2, F8)   **$$$$+**
French
Relive the Indochine experience Singapore-style with upper-crust French fare such as foie gras and truffles plus surprise transcontinental interlopers such as tiramisu, ocean trout ceviche and Iranian caviar. Dress to match the surrounds: a historic colonial building with terrace featuring polished boards, Oriental carpets, a huge chandelier and delightful views of the Botanic Gardens and river. Bookings and gold credit card are recommended.
✉ **EJH Corner House, Singapore Botanic Gardens, Cluny Rd** ☎ **6466 8812** 🚌 **7, 77, 106, 123, 174** ⏱ serving hours: Mon-Fri noon-2pm, Mon-Sun 7-9pm

Bobby Rubinos
(3, H6)   **$$**
American Grill
Apparently this is the place for ribs – put some meat on yours with reasonably priced burgers, grills and other carnivorous delights. Happy-hour beer, a pool table and breezy courtyard eating by the fountain should keep you amused.
✉ **#B1-03 Fountain Court, Chijmes, 30 Victoria St** ☎ **6337 5477** Ⓜ **City Hall** ⏱ noon-10.30pm ♿

Café Les Amis
(2, F8)   **$**
Cafe
Enjoy breezy outdoor eating in the botanic gardens surrounded by waving greenery, water fountains and the odd fluffy-tailed squirrel. The coffee's not great, but try the reasonably priced set breakfast, a local special or pastry, over a newspaper.
✉ **Gateway Complex, Singapore Botanic Gardens, Cluny Rd** ☎ **6467 7326** 🚌 **7, 77, 106, 123, 174** ⏱ 7.30am-7.30pm ♿

China Jump (3, H6) **$$**
American Grill
Holy China Jumping ostrich steaks, Batman! You can get one for $26. Unleash your hunger and rip into one along with lashings of

Take a break from chopsticks and try the tapas at Ochos, olé!

happy, happy-hour beer. Or try the Tex-Mex fare.

✉ **#B1-07/08 Chijmes, 30 Victoria St** ☎ **6338 9388** Ⓜ **City Hall** ⏲ **5-10.30pm** ☼

Halia (Ginger) Restaurant (2, F8) $$
Eastern/Continental
Set amid the recently planted ginger garden this newcomer sits neatly between its neighbours in terms of price and atmosphere. Feast on house specials such as a seafood stew perfumed with ginger blossoms or tuck into a linguine of baby black mussels. Inside relax amid air-con and natural timbers or soak up the sun on the deck outdoors.

✉ **Ginger Garden, Singapore Botanic Gardens, Cluny Rd (enter via Tyersall Ave)** ☎ **6476 6711** 🚌 **7, 77, 106, 123, 174** ⏲ **11am-11pm, Sat-Sun breakfast buffet 8-10.30am** ☼ **some children's portions available on request**

Lei Garden (3, H6) $$$
Hong Kong Cantonese
Reservations are essential at this popular yet elegant eatery featuring a wall-length fish tank and dozens of round tables packed with business types and Chinese families out for a special occasion. Speciality shark fin, double-boiled herbal soups and some abalone dishes need one to three days pre-ordering. Dim sum is a winner with lunchtime crowds.

✉ **#01-24 Chijmes, 30 Victoria St** ☎ **6339 3822** Ⓜ **City Hall** ⏲ **11.30am-2.30pm, 6-10pm** ☼

Maison de Fontaine (3, H6) $$$
French
We're not sure why a Caesar salad is lurking on the menu, but this place gets the thumbs up from Singapore's gourmet literati. Try the baked crabmeat cream soup with Armagnac or a traditional Provencale rack of lamb. The indoor decor is a little twee but the courtyard makes for balmy dining.

✉ **#01-26/27 Caldwell House, Chijmes, 30 Victoria St** ☎ **6336 0286** Ⓜ **City Hall** ⏲ **noon-2.30pm, 6.30-10pm**

Ochos (3, H6) $$
Spanish Tapas Bar
If you're having nightmares about being chased by a giant pair of chopsticks trying to lasso you with a rope of noodles, it might be time to change your diet. Tapas is a fun way to share food with friends – and you can use a fork. Try the spicy grilled prawns and *patatas bravas*, rounded off with Spanish rice pudding.

✉ **#01-12/13/14 Chijmes, 30 Victoria St** ☎ **6883 1508** Ⓜ **City Hall** ⏲ **noon-3pm, 6.30-10pm; bar closes Sun-Thurs 1am, Fri-Sat 2am** ☼ Ⓥ

Original Sin (2, F7) $$
Vegetarian
This is possibly Singapore's only upmarket vegetarian restaurant. Expect Mediterranean staples like bruschettas and pizzas plus a fabulous array of changing specials. Good service and yummy food make reservations essential.

✉ **Blk 43, #01-62 Jalan Merah Saga, Chip Bee**

Late Eats
While hawker stalls are open from dawn till dark, most restaurants have irritatingly short serving hours – sometimes it's all over by 9pm. Don't go to bed on a grumbling tummy. Try the nearest hawker food centre, or head to **Samlor** (p. 85), **Chatterbox** (p. 80) or **Newton Food Centre** (p. 75), all of which are open 24hrs. Other good bets include **Sultan 8** (p. 87), **Five Star Hainanese Chicken Rice** (p. 90) and **Rossi Restaurant** (p. 79), all open till late.

Gardens, Holland Village ☎ **6475 5605** Ⓜ **Buona Vista** ⏲ **Tues-Sun 11.30am-2.30pm, 6.30pm-late** Ⓥ

Tatsu Sushi (3, H6) $$
Japanese
This is ideal for solo diners – sit along the bench for front-row views of the knife-slicing/rice-rolling action by the resident chef and the gracious attentions of kimono-clad waitresses. The giant clam steam sets and the tuna with Japanese yam sure are tempting.

✉ **#01-16 Block F, The Gallery, Chijmes, 30 Victoria St** ☎ **6332 5868** Ⓜ **City Hall** ⏲ **noon-3pm, 6.30-10.30pm**

EAST COAST

Five Star Hainanese Chicken Rice

(5, D5) $

Chinese Stall

'You want chicken rice?' is the standard greeting here – to which you should nod 'Yes, please!' and order a lime juice. Two minutes later you'll be tucking into fast food that's actually worth waiting for.

✉ 191 East Coast Rd
☎ 6344 5911
Ⓜ Eunos then taxi
🕙 11am-2am ♿

Hock Heng Teochow Porridge

(5, B4) $

Chinese Stall

Mmm...even the Famous Five's picnic basket would find it hard to compete with this lunchtime spread. Choose from fresh blue swimmer crabs, silvery pan-fried fishes with garlic and chilli, fresh greens or marinated tofu.

✉ 39 Joo Chiat Pl
☎ 6348 0239 Ⓜ Eunos then taxi 🕙 10am-10pm ♿ Ⓥ

Just Greens Vegetarian Food

(5, B4) $

Vegetarian

You know the vegetarian food is kosher when you're knocking elbows with Buddhist monks. Check out the soaking fungi at the entrance.

✉ 49/51 Joo Chiat Pl
☎ 6345 0069 Ⓜ Eunos then taxi 🕙 10am-10pm ♿ Ⓥ

Katong Bakery & Confectionary

(5, D4) $

Nonya Cafe

This pre-WWII Nonya cake and coffee shop is still serving up cream rolls, dark honey cakes and fluffy sponges in original surrounds – marble-topped tables and rickety wooden chairs. If they aren't already heritage listed we'd like to nominate the whole shop, including the recipes and the sweet, grey-haired proprietor, as national treasures.

✉ 75 East Coast Rd
Ⓜ Eunos then taxi
🕙 11.30am-8pm ♿ Ⓥ

Long Beach Seafood Restaurant

(2, G11) $$

Seafood

Locals pack this place out for its famous black pepper crabs and live 'drunken prawns' soaked in brandy. It's potentially messy but definitely fun.

✉ 1018 East Coast Parkway ☎ 6445 8833
🚌 16 (cross via underpass), 36 🕙 11am-3pm, 5pm-midnight ♿

Mango Tree

(2, G11) $$$

Indian

This tasteful, waterfront restaurant pulls crowds across town with its reputation for excellent Indian cuisine. Start off with a pepper and tamarind soup before rolling up your sleeves for the crab masala. Squeeze in a cooling mango sorbet for dessert then walk it off with a (long) stroll on the beach.

✉ 1000 East Coast Parkway ☎ 6442 8655
🚌 16 (cross via underpass), 36
🕙 noon-2.30pm, 6-10pm

No Signboard Seafood

(5, B1) $$

Seafood

Lots of locals stop by for a reasonably priced seafood extravaganza at this simple eatery with outdoor tables. Try the chilli crab.

✉ 414 Geylang Rd
☎ 6842 3415
Ⓜ Aljunied
🕙 3pm-2am ♿

Porridge King Restaurant

(5, D5) $

Peranakan, Chinese & Fusion

Antiques collector, handyman and sometime underwear model Alvin Koh is onto a winner with his Porridge King restaurants, which serve up reliable fare based on his grandma's favourite recipes. Fusing Zen minimalism with an African theme, the King is perhaps a little too eclectic for his own good, but who cares? Try the century egg congee or grandma's stir-fried 'crystal' seafood *horfun*.

✉ 205 East Coast Rd
☎ 6440 8738 Ⓜ Eunos then taxi 🕙 Mon-Fri 11am-11pm, Sat-Sun 9am-11pm ♿

Spoons

(2, G11) $$$

Eastern & Mediterranean

There's no seaside view here but Spoons does a damn good gnocchi and divine rare duck salad in slick but unsurprising surroundings. Indulging in a tipple or two could send you over budget.

✉ #01-11, 86 East Coast Rd ☎ 6345 4994
Ⓜ Eunos then taxi
🕙 noon-2.30pm, 6-10pm

entertainment

Singapore's nightlife gets a bad rap, but mainly from people who have ill-advisedly spent their time swilling over-priced Singapore Slings in dubious hotel lobbies. There's no excuse for an early night in Singapore, most nights you'll find a groovy bar for a drink or a club where you can bust some moves. With the recession, clubs and bars in Singapore have been doing it tough, but that hasn't stemmed the flow of new ventures.

Clubs in Singapore close at 3am and of course, the island is strictly a drug-free zone, but the club scene boasts great local acts and Singapore is a regular stop-off for international touring DJs. In contrast the live music scene is fairly dismal; cover bands, muzak-flavoured jazz and tinkling piano classics of the Richard Clayderman variety rule the day.

Singaporeans love the movies – but screenings are usually mainstream US blockbusters. However, the city does have an exciting and vibrant theatre scene staging everything from experimental original works to repertory standards. You'll also find plenty of classical and tourist-friendly opera performances.

Singapore is keen to promote itself as an arts destination and while the government's motives may be questionable (like PAP Minister George Yeo's memorable announcement that 'fun is serious business'), it can only have interesting results.

Tickets for most productions are available through SISTIC (☎ 6348 5555; e www.sistic.com.sg) and TicketCharge (☎ 6296 2929).

For the latest news and listings read *The Straits Times* newspaper, *Eight Days* and the *Arts Magazine*. For nightlife check out free street press *I-S Magazine* and *Juice*, *Pulp* and *Big O*, available at cafes, hotels, music and some clothes shops.

Top Spots

Mohamed Sultan Rd is *the* strip for big bars and nightclubs, Orchard Rd is populated mainly by hotel and franchise-style bars and mainstream clubs, Chinatown is home to an eclectic range of small bars and restaurants in shophouses, Boat Quay is loud and a little trashy while the colonial area offers patches of nightlife at the **One Fullerton** (opposite the Fullerton Hotel), **Equinox** (Swissôtel), **Victoria Theatre & Concert Hall** (p. 27) and **Raffles** (p. 29) with the **Esplanade – Theatres on the Bay** (pp. 20-1) complex not far away.

Think pinkk! Cruise Chinatown's bars.

SPECIAL EVENTS

January-February *Ponggal* – harvest thanksgiving festival celebrated by South Indians, especially at the Sri Mariamman Temple (p. 35)

Chinese New Year – dragon dances and pedestrian parades in Chinatown

Chingay – processions of lion dancers, floats and Chinese flag bearers parade down Orchard Rd

Thaipusam – Hindu devotees march from the Sri Srinivasa Perumal carrying *kavadis*, decorated metal frames, hung from metal hooks and spikes driven into their flesh

Hari Raya Puasa – marks the end of Ramadan, the month-long Muslim fast, with three days of celebration; in the Malay areas, Geylang Serai is draped in lights

March-April *Qing Ming Festival* – 'All Souls' Day'; Chinese visit the tombs of their ancestors to clean and repair them and make offerings

Hari Raya Haji – Muslim festival honouring those who have made the pilgrimage to Mecca; prayers are said at mosques throughout the city

April-May *Vesak Day* – Buddha's birth, enlightenment and death are celebrated with various events, including the release of caged birds to symbolise the setting free of captive souls

May-June *Birthday of the Third Prince* – the Chinese child-god is honoured with processions, and devotees go into a trance and spear themselves with spikes and swords.

Dragon Boat Festival – boat races across Marina Bay

Singapore Festival of Arts – world-class event held every even-numbered year

Festival of Asian Performing Arts – held every odd-numbered year

July-August *Singapore Food Festival* – month-long festival

Great Singapore Sale – centred on Orchard Rd for one month usually overlapping with the food festival

Singapore National Day – 9 August; military and civilian processions and fireworks celebrate Singapore's independence

Festival of the Hungry Ghosts – the souls of the dead are released for feasting and entertainment on earth

September-October *Birthday of the Monkey God* – celebrated twice a year at the Monkey God Temple (p. 42); mediums pierce their cheeks and tongues with skewers

Thimithi (Fire-Walking Ceremony) – Hindu devotees prove their faith by walking across glowing coals at the Sri Mariamman Temple (p. 35)

Moon-Cake Festival – the overthrow of the Mongol warlords in ancient China is celebrated by eating moon cakes and lighting colourful paper lanterns

Navarathri – the 'Nine Nights' festival is dedicated to the wives of Shiva, Vishnu and Brahma and celebrated at Indian temples with young girls are dressed as the goddess Kali

October-November *Pilgrimage to Kusu Island* – Tua Pek Kong, the god of prosperity, is honoured by Taoists

Deepavali – Little India is ablaze with lights for a month during this most important Hindu festival

Festival of the Nine Emperor Gods – nine days of Chinese operas, processions and other events

BARS & PUBS

Alley Bar (4, B8)
Squeezed into an undercover alley and attached to a renovated shophouse on Emerald Hill is Alley Bar, a slick new wine/dim-sum bar that's taken the place of what used to be the Peranakan Showcase Museum. Some of the museum's artefacts are still on display so now drinking, smoking and lounging about can be an educational experience.
✉ 2 Emerald Hill Rd ☎ 6235 9810 Ⓜ Orchard ⏲ Sun-Thur 5pm-2am, Fri-Sat 5pm-3am

Altivo Bar & Lounge (2, H8) By day you can enjoy a cold beer and fine views from Mt Faber, but at night the retro-style lounge bar action starts up with funky tunes, disco moves and loads of mini skirts.
✉ Mt Faber ☎ 6270 8223 e www.altivo.com.sg 🚋 from World Trade Centre ⏲ bar: 1-7pm; lounge: 7pm-3am

Balaclava (3, H8)
Imagine yourself in a Soviet-inspired 1960s party HQ, puffing on a cigar and shouting the bar with hideously expensive French champagne. Live jazz provides ear candy and staff are easy on the eye. Now imagine said bunker attached to an enormous pastel-painted convention and shopping centre... suspend disbelief. There's an over-25 age limit.
✉ 01-01B Singapore Convention Centre, 1 Raffles Blvd ☎ 6339 1600 Ⓜ City Hall 🚌 97, 124, 167, 174 ⏲ Mon-Thur noon-midnight, Fri-Sat noon-2am, Sun 4pm-midnight $ occasional cover charge for jazz events

Going Solo

Singaporeans are a pretty friendly bunch so it isn't hard to strike up conversation and because it's so safe you won't feel uneasy being alone. Club St in Chinatown offers some cosy eating and drinking options and you won't feel conspicuous dining alfresco at Chijmes. You may meet other tourists at the bars along Emerald Hill, off Orchard Rd. For dancing the **Liquid Room** (p. 96) and **Velvet Underground** (p. 95) clubs are smaller than the cavernous venues on Mohamed Sultan Rd.

Go it alone in the outdoors at Chijmes.

Bar at the Box
(3, M5) This designer bar and art gallery just off Club St is a collaboration between Wong San's and Art Season's galleries and hosts arty events from exhibitions to poetry readings. Enjoy martinis, tasty Japanese bar snacks and chocolates.
✉ 5 Gemmill La ☎ 6327 1276 Ⓜ Raffles Place ⏲ Mon-Fri 11am-3pm, 5pm-midnight; Sat 11am-3pm, 5pm-1am; Sun 3pm-midnight

Bar Opiume (3, K6)
A gleaming glass bar, square stainless steel and leather furniture and exposed pipes contrast with the polished boards, massive chandeliers and the bar's genteel environs in a colonial building fronting the water opposite Boat Quay. Indochine's latest bar is a glasshouse – or a fish bowl – see and be seen.
✉ Empress Place ☎ 6339 3876 Ⓜ Raffles Place ⏲ 6pm-late

Bar Sa Vanh (3, M5)
By night the bar is filled with glowing lights and dusky shadows, gorgeous svelte things flit by the goldfish pond, ex-pats guzzle beer from sunken lounges, platters of Asian tapas make the rounds, chilling tunes snake into the night – all under the watchful eyes of Buddha himself.
✉ 49A Club St ☎ 6323 0145 Ⓜ Raffles Place ⏲ 6pm-late

Davis Café (3, M4)

This laid-back Bali-inspired cafe-cum-drinking-hole next to the night hawker stalls is pitching itself at the backpacker crowd. It claims to make a killer Singapore Sling.

✉ 28 Smith St ☎ 6220 9390 Ⓜ Outram Park ◷ noon-11pm

The Dubliner (4, C9)

Bad Irish pubs filled with boozy ex-pats are ubiquitous in Singapore. This one gets a mention because it's situated in a lovely, white colonial building with a breezy beer-friendly verandah. If you're hungry try its good pub grub.

✉ Winsland Conservation House, 165 Penang Rd ☎ 6735 2220 Ⓜ Somerset ◷ meals: noon-2.30pm, 6.30-10.00pm

Embargo @ Centro

(3, K7) Enjoy wine, tapas and designer views at Embargo before heading upstairs inside Centro to the cigar lounge. Dress to impress.

✉ One Fullerton, 1 Fullerton Rd ☎ 6220 2288 ℮ www.centro 360.com Ⓜ Raffles Place ◷ Sun-Wed 5pm-2am, Thur-Sat 5pm-3am

5 Emerald Hill (4, B8)

This is a long-running cocktail & wine bar with Asiatic touches and a pool table upstairs. The surrounds are a little twee but it still beats Orchard Rd and you'll need a drink after all that shopping.

✉ 5 Emerald Hill Rd ☎ 6732 0818 Ⓜ Somerset ◷ Mon-Sat noon-late, Sun 5pm-late

---

Ex-pats

In pre-handover Hong Kong they used to call them FILTH (Failed in London Try Hong Kong), but Singapore has plenty of *ang mo* of its own, lured by ex-pat packages and the government's Foreign Talent program. They even have their own magazine *Expat* – 'Living Well is the Best Revenge'. Ex-pats are typically (if not fairly) stereotyped as earning heaps of money and hanging around in their condo swimming pools while bitching about their maids, taxi drivers and everything else in Singapore. These neo-colonialists may have ditched the pith helmet for a laptop but they still succumb to tropical diseases, such as 'yellow fever' – the term used to describe newly arrived ex-pat boys chasing local women. The best place to experience this strange singles scene is the multitiered theme bars at Orchard Towers (400 Orchard Rd; 4, B3) charmingly nicknamed the 'Four Floors of Whores'.

Ice Cold Beer (4, B8)

In an old shophouse, this pub features drunk locals, drunker ex-pats and lots of really cold beer. It hardly makes for a refined atmosphere, but do you care? Perhaps not.

✉ 9 Emerald Hill Rd ☎ 6735 9929 Ⓜ Somerset ◷ 6pm-late

Le Bar (3, K4)

In a 120-year-old building, Le Bar fuses soaring ceilings, original antique scrolls and black lacquer-look furniture with '80s neon lighting like a time-warping cyber-punk set – if only Keanu Reeves would turn up at happy hour.

✉ Asian Restaurant and Bar, 50 Eu Tong Sen St (enter at New Market Rd) ☎ 6534 6006 🚌 63, 124, 174, 197 ◷ noon-late

Milk Bar (3, J2)

This is a top little spot – it's small, round, groovy in a low-key kind of way and

---

there's a dance floor upstairs. Stop in for drinks and a game of Scrabble while you treat your ears to a vibey House massage.

✉ #01-09 Gallery Hotel, 76 Robertson Quay ☎ 6836 4431 🚌 65, 139, 970 ◷ 6pm-3am

New Asia Bar & Grill

(3, H7) Featuring a giant, curving mother-of-pearl wall, soaring ceilings, a VIP mezzanine, a dance floor that tilts a tricky 20 degrees, and the most spectacular views in Singapore, this bar is hardly a shrinking violet.

✉ L71-72, Equinox, Swissôtel, 2 Stamford Rd ☎ 6837 3322 ℮ www.equinoxcom plex.com Ⓜ City Hall ◷ Sun-Thur 11.30am-1am, Fri-Sat 11.30am-3am

Pinkk (3, M5)

Pink lights, pink chairs, pink drinks in (no, you're not imagining it) ever so slightly slanted glasses. This bar is a bit like *I Dream of Jeanie*'s boudoir, but with corners. And without 'Master' bossing you around all the time when you're busy trying to get drunk. Models night Thursday!

✉ **44/46 Club St**
☎ **6221 3466**
Ⓜ **Raffles Place**
🕐 **5pm-3am**
Ⓢ **occasional cover charge**

Post Bar (3, K7)

Located in the swish Fullerton Hotel this former post office boasts high ceilings and Art Deco-like metallic finishes. Mid-week you might find it home to hotel guests in off-duty businessmen garb (khakis and loafers). Things get better-looking at the weekend.

✉ **Fullerton Hotel, 1 Fullerton Sq** ☎ **6733 8388** e **www.fullerton hotel.com** Ⓜ **Raffles Place** 🕐 **Mon-Fri noon-2am, Sat 5pm-3am, Sun brunch noon-2pm (bookings essential)**

SClub (3, G7)

It's white, loud and full of booze – at least it's a bar and not your boss. Work off some post-Purvis St calories with some funky moves.

✉ **11 Purvis St** ☎ **6339 5098** Ⓜ **City Hall**
🕐 **8pm-late**

Sound Bar (3, J2)

Choose between alfresco riverside frontage and hanging out on bar stools by the glowing fish tank. Chilling tunes, evening breezes and a cute clientele make for a pleasant evening. Later you can check out the Liquid Room club upstairs (see p. 96) –

or if you're feeling especially lucky, book a hotel room and stay the night.

✉ **Gallery Hotel, 76 Robertson Quay**
☎ **6333 8117**
e **www.liquidroom .com.sg** 🚌 **65, 139, 970** 🕐 **Wed-Sat 11pm-3am**

Tangos (2, F7)

Pleasant, verandah style bar/eatery with white interior, fans and soothing lighting. Located in ex-pat heaven, Holland Village, it's not worth crossing town for but is a good option compared to the neighbouring franchises.

✉ **35 Lorong Mambong, Holland Village** ☎ **6463 7364**
🚌 **77, 106, 174**
🕐 **6pm-late** ♿

two rooms (3, H3)

Singapore's bright young things pose over martinis and suck down big daddy cigars interspersed with hits of flavoured oxygen from boutique-sized tanks which glow intriguingly by the luminescent bar. OK, it's a little silly, but who cares?

✉ **207 River Valley Rd**
☎ **6735 6193**
🚌 **65, 139, 970**
🕐 **Mon-Sat 7pm-3am**

Union Bar (3, M5)

With big squishy retro

couches, plenty of room and views onto happening Club St, this place is hard to beat for a relaxed beer or two. Chill out.

✉ **81 Club St**
☎ **6327 4990**
Ⓜ **Raffles Place**
🕐 **Mon-Thur 5pm-1am, Fri-Sun 5pm-2am**

Velvet Underground (3, J1)

This Moroccan-inspired bar features multi-coloured club lounges, gold banquettes and a real Keith Haring painting. It's a classy joint and to get in you'd better look a treat and pack some cash. Expect to hear New York vibe, garage and commercial dance. Age limit 28+.

✉ **Zouk, 17 Jiak Kim St** ☎ **6738 2988**
e **www.zoukclub.com**
🕐 **Tues-Sat 9pm-3am**
Ⓢ **$35, includes two drinks & entry to Zouk & Phuture (p. 97)**

Zouk Wine Bar (3, J1)

Stop by for pre-Zouk club drinks and cocktails at this alfresco wine bar, which lacks the designer vibe of the clubs next door but does offer views onto all manner of riverside shenanigans.

✉ **Zouk, 17 Jiak Kim St** ☎ **6738 2988**
e **www.zoukclub.com**
🕐 **7pm-3am**

Keith Haring on display at the Velvet Underground.

CLUBS

Clubs in Singapore are forever folding and revamping, one of the best ways to figure out what's hot and what's not is by leafing through street press; try *I-S Magazine*, *Juice* and *Pulp* for the latest reviews. Cover charges can be hefty, but they usually include a free drink or two. Happy hours and 'women drink for free' promotions are ubiquitous. Sentosa Island hosts an outdoor rave once a year and regular Black Moon foam parties (call ☎ 1800 736 8672 for details).

Centro (3, K7)

Singapore's hottest new bar, club and restaurant complex is even giving Zouk a run for its money. Spread over 20,000 sq ft and boasting sleek multitiered design, floor-to-ceiling glass windows, killer river views and a giant raised dance platform, this place is not messing around. DJ dignitaries such as Nick Warren and Dimitri from Paris have performed here. Boys' night Sundays. Age 21+.
⊠ **One Fullerton, 1 Fullerton Rd** ☎ **6220 2288** e **www.centro 360.com** ⊘ **Tues-Sun 9pm-3am** Ⓜ **Raffles Place** Ⓢ **variable**

Drugs Are Bad

If you want to arrive back home in one piece don't even think about taking drugs in Singapore. Like neighbouring states Singapore imposes the death penalty for trafficking, importing and exporting even relatively small amounts of illegal drugs. Not funny, lah.

China Black (4, B4)

Previously known as Venom, this place has enjoyed the kind of Eastern-inspired makeover that's sweeping Singapore. With a mix of commercial dance, top 40 and R&B the crowd is predictably mainstream.
⊠ **#12 Pacific Plaza Penthouse, 9 Scotts Rd** ☎ **6734 7677** Ⓜ **Orchard** ⊘ **Mon-Fri 5pm-3am, Sat 7pm-3am, Sun 9pm-3am**

Club Eden (3, H3)

One of the best along this strip, this club boasts slick design, deep House grooves and two bars – no bottlenecks. The curvy white booths are ideal for perving at the Adams and Eves on the dance floor, but the DJ's mix won't let you sit still for long.
⊠ **25 Mohamed Sultan Rd** ☎ **6738 0720** e **www.edensingapore .com** 🚌 **65, 139, 970** ⊘ **6pm-3am** Ⓢ **variable**

Liquid Room (3, J2)

Less liquid and more gunmetal, this surprisingly small club has an industrial feel. With some of Singapore's best DJ line-ups – including culture jammer X'Ho – this is the spot for serious dance. Get down to progressive House, tech-House and trance – if you can make it past the queue. Unfortunately, with so few toilets inside you might find yourself jigging around and crossing your legs regardless of the music.
⊠ **Gallery Hotel, 76 Robertson Quay** ☎ **6333 8117** e **www .liquidroom.com.sg** 🚌 **65, 139, 970** ⊘ **10pm-late** Ⓢ **variable**

Madam Wongs

(3, H3) It's looking a bit tired around the edges but this Shanghai-inspired retro and top 40 club is still packing in crowds of bopping youngsters slugging their beers and mooning around mawkishly in their loved one's arms.
⊠ **12 Mohamed Sultan Rd** ☎ **6738 4024** e **www.wongsans.com** 🚌 **65, 139, 970** ⊘ **3pm-3am** Ⓢ **Fri-Sat $17**

Nuerhong (3, F6)

This big, loud, slightly trashy but fun Oriental-themed pub and disco plays mainstream and retro tunes. The upstairs wine bar is supposed to offer a tasteful retreat.
⊠ **81 Bencoolen St** ☎ **6837 3740** Ⓜ **Dhoby Ghaut** ⊘ **6pm-late**

Orange (3, H3)

Commercial R&B and top 40 tunes are the order of the night at this loud, orange and purple cavernous club that's easy to lose yourself in. Notable features are the O-shaped bar, orange pool table and weekend queues that trail out onto the road.

✉ #01-03, 33 Mohamed Sultan Rd ☎ 6734 4680 🚌 65, 139, 970 🕐 Mon-Sat 7pm-3am ⑤ variable

Phuture (3, J1)

'Phuturistic' design featuring lava lamps and stainless steel provide the backdrop for Zouk youngsters tripping and hopping to trip-hop and old school drum & bass beats. Age limit 18+.

✉ Zouk, 17 Jiak Kim St ☎ 6738 2988 e www.zoukclub.com 🕐 Wed-Sat 7pm-3am ⑤ $10-25, Fri-Sat $12 before 9pm (includes entry to Zouk)

Zouk (3, J1)

This is the original Ibiza-inspired club which has made Zouk an international name and a regu-lar destination for five-star international DJs. With five bars and a roomy dance floor there's guaranteed drinking access and plenty of space to strut your stuff. UK's DJ bible *Muzik* magazine gave the ultimate stamp of approval when it released a mix by Zouk's resident DJ Aldrin.

✉ 17 Jiak Kim St ☎ 6738 2988 e www.zoukclub.com 🕐 Wed-Sat 7pm-3am ⑤ $25 (Zouk entry only)

Spectator Sports

Most large-scale sports and entertainment events – from pop concerts and soccer games to celebrity wrestling – take place at **Singapore Indoor Stadium** (2 Stadium Walk; 2, G10; ☎ 6344 2660; e www.singaporeindoorstadium.com; Ⓜ Kallang then 🚌 11). Check its website or *The Straits Times*.

Night horse races are held Wednesdays (7.15pm), Saturdays (6pm) and some Sundays at the **Singapore Turf Club** (1 Turf Club Ave; 2, B6; ☎ 6879 1000, e www.turfclub.com.sg, Ⓜ Kranji). There is a four-level grandstand with a seating capacity of up to 35,000. Admission costs $5 ($10 air-con). For $20 tourists can access the air-conditioned gold card room; a passport is required. Dress code is collared shirt and pants for men and women must wear closed shoes (no sandals). All betting is government controlled and the minimum win or place bet is $5. See also Organised Tours, p. 60-1, for package deals.

Pssst…the word on the street press is it'll tell you where to strut your stuff.

GAY & LESBIAN SINGAPORE

Adrenalin Sports Bar
(3, F5) Some business-minded air crew dared to dream – this is what they came up with: an unlikely-sounding venue which has become a popular G&L haunt thanks to the cheap drinks, a ladies-only pool night on Wednesdays and the odd pack of peanuts.
✉ #01-02, 40 Prinsep St ☎ 6336 0718
Ⓜ Dhoby Ghaut
🕐 6pm-late

Backstage Bar
(3, M4) Don't be put off by the 'PLU Members Only' sign downstairs – friends of the rainbow flag have automatic membership. This is a cosy little mens pub and a great spot to chat (and flirt) with locals. If you want to dance but don't have your gear there's a clubbing boutique upstairs for Cinderella-like transformations.
✉ 13A Trengganu St

(entrance up the stairs on Temple St)
☎ 6227 1712
Ⓜ Outram Park
🕐 7pm-2am ⑤ free

Dbl O (3, J3)
It's not strictly a lesbian and gay bar but locals says that on weekends you can barely move for flying sequins and camouflage army gear. The club likes to keep its patrons guessing with regular theme nights and matching decor changes, but hopefully your fellow patrons won't keep you guessing for long.
✉ #02-21 Robertson Walk, 11 Unity St
☎ 6735 2008
🄴 www.dbl-O.com
🚌 65, 139, 970
🕐 Wed-Sat 8pm-3am
⑤ $15/25 after 10pm, includes 2 drinks

Mad Monks (3, J5)
It's hard to believe but this vaguely medieval-themed

pub on the waterfront hosts girls nights Thurs-Sat. Head down for a beer or two and try and coax those Singaporean princesses out from their shining armour.
✉ #B1-01/06 Riverwalk, 20 Upper Circular Rd
Ⓜ Raffles Place
🕐 Thurs-Sat 6pm-late

Niche Café & Pub
(3, M4) The entrance looks a little dubious but upstairs you'll find there's nothing more sinister than guys in black leather pants lip-synching to Kylie Minogue. Boys and girls welcome. Attracts a younger crowd.
✉ 32A Pagoda St
☎ 6323 6063
🄴 www.members.tripod.com/niche_pub
Ⓜ Raffles Place
🕐 Tues-Sat 9pm-3am

Taboo Café & Bar
(3, N4) The rules are no kissing or taking your T-shirt off but thankfully that doesn't seem to stop anyone. Tabu is mostly a boys club but girls are welcome. Be aware that this place has been targeted for 'overcrowding'.
✉ #01-04, 21 Tanjong Pagar Rd ☎ 6225 4172 Ⓜ Tanjong Pagar
🕐 varies ⑤ cover charge Sat-Sun

Why Not? (3, N4)
Plant yourself on a podium and shake that booty for all its worth. One of Singapore's most popular G&L hangouts boasts non-stop House and crowd-pleaser anthems.
✉ 56/58 Tras St
☎ 6323 3010 Ⓜ Tanjong Pagar 🕐 8pm-late

Gay & Lesbian Singapore

Homosexuality in Singapore is still illegal, yet actual persecution is rare and officials tend to turn a blind eye. Crackdowns on venues are extremely rare, but while unlikely they *are* possible. Most of the gay and lesbian scene is centred in the Chinatown and Tanjong Pagar area. There's no lesbian bar in Singapore but you'll find women-only nights at venues such as **Zouk** (p. 97) and the **Liquid Room** (p. 96), also keep an eye out for events by Club Herstory or subscribe to the Flower Party mailing list (🄴 flowerparty@email.com).

Boys should go to **'Centro Boyz'** night on Sundays (p. 96), **Zouk** (p. 97) on Wednesdays and **Orange** (p. 96) on Thursdays. **Babylon Karaoke** (52 Tanjong Pagar Rd; 3, N4; ☎ 6222 8462) is also popular.

The best way to find out what's happening is to check 🄴 www.fridae.com for the girls and 🄴 www.sgboy.com for the boys. You'll also find queer cabaret at the **Boom Boom Room** (p. 101).

LIVE MUSIC

Unlike the club scene, live music is not a happening thang in Singapore. It's hard to find local bands (try *Big O* magazine; **e** www.bigo.com.sg) and even when you do it's most likely that they'll be playing covers. Cover bands ranging from reggae to salsa perform at hotel restaurants, including **Blu** (Shangri-La, p. 80), **Brix** (Hyatt, p. 104) and **Bar None** (Marriott, p. 106). Regular music events also take place at **Fort Canning** and **Chijmes**.

Crazy Elephant

(3, J4) Down by the waterside, Singapore's best blues bar offers beer, blokes and blues. All of which make for a loud, enthusiastic atmosphere where testosterone is in plentiful supply.
✉ **#01-06/07 Traders Market, 3E River Valley Rd, Clarke Quay**
☎ **6337 1990** **e** **www .crazyelephant.com**
🚌 **65, 139, 970**
🕐 **6pm-late**

Fat Frog Café **(3, H5)**

This cafe at the Substation arts house is one of the only places you'll catch local bands in action. Bands play outside in the courtyard on weekends; if you're lucky you might catch something interesting.
✉ **45 Armenian St**
☎ **6338 6201** **Ⓜ** **City Hall** 🚌 **97, 124, 167**
🕐 **Sun-Thur 11.30am-11pm, Fri-Sat 11.30am-1am**

Harry's Bar **(3, L6)**

At the quiet, grown-ups' end of Boat Quay, Harry's Bar offers some relief from the mismatched cacophony at the other end and the jazz goes well with nighttime city views. Despite the international line-up all the ex-pats and tourists hanging around don't really lend it a happening vibe.
✉ **28 Boat Quay**
☎ **6538 3029**
Ⓜ **Raffles Place**
🕐 **11am-late, shows from 10pm**

OD's Backstage Music Bar **(2, G10)**

Out at Stadium Cove, OD's offers alfresco riverside drinks outside and predictable, but pretty good local blues and jazz cover bands inside. The outside seating provides an appealing escape route when it gets too loud.
✉ **#01-07 Singapore Indoor Stadium, 2 Stadium Walk**
Ⓜ **Kallang then bus 11** 🚌 **11, 16, 608**
🕐 **Sun-Thur 6pm-1am, Fri-Sat 5pm-2am**

Top Ten

Singapore's pub scene is not particularly supportive of local musicians. The best venues to catch local acts are at the Substation's Fat Frog Café and the Youth Park (p. 48). Local band favourites include: Force Vomit, The Oddfellows, Stomping Ground, The Boredphucks, The Padres, Urban Karma, etc, Chou Ji Piang plus muso/DJs Paul T and X-Ho.

Roomful of Blues

(3, F5) You can expect to hear blues and reggae at this bar; one of the few that supports Singapore's floundering local music scene.
✉ **72 Prinsep St**
☎ **6837 0882**
Ⓜ **Dhoby Ghaut**
🕐 **11.30am-2am**

Somerset **(3, H7)**

This place reputably boasts the best jazz in Singapore – unfortunately it comes with a shopping mall location and beige hotel lobby ambience.
✉ **L3, Raffles the Plaza, 2 Stamford Rd**
☎ **6338 8585** **Ⓜ** **City Hall** 🕐 **5pm-2am**

Check out Chijmes for live music.

DANCE & CLASSICAL MUSIC

Chinese Theatre Circle (3, M4)

This Chinese opera company produces traditional operas – complete with full costume and make-up – in Chinese and English. In addition to major productions you can also enjoy tea, performances and cultural sessions here daily.

✉ 5 Smith St ☎ 6323 4862; tickets through SISTIC 6348 5555
Ⓜ Outram Park

Nrityalaya Aesthetics Society (3, F6)

This educational and performing arts body features Singapore's only full-time Indian dance troop and a host of classical Indian musicians. It attracted mainstream attention recently with its ancient Sanskrit production of *Shakuntala* with English voice-over. It holds an annual drama festival.

✉ #01-01 Stamford Arts Centre, 155 Waterloo St ☎ 6336 6537; tickets through SISTIC ℮ www.nas .org.sg Ⓜ Bugis

Singapore Chinese Orchestra (3, O5)

Experience classical Chinese music and traditional instruments with Singapore's best Chinese orchestra. The orchestra sometimes offers free performances in parks and community centres – check the website for details.

✉ Singapore Conference Hall, 7 Shenton Way ☎ 6557 4034 or SISTIC ℮ www.sco -music.org.sg
Ⓜ Tanjong Pagar

Singapore Dance Theatre (3, G5)

Founded in 1988 the Singapore Dance Theatre company produces traditional ballet favourites (*Giselle*, *The Nutcracker* etc) alongside contemporary works including those of the late Singaporean choreographer Goh Choo San. Don't miss its Ballet Under the Stars season at Fort Canning.

✉ #02 Fort Canning Centre, Cox Terrace ☎ tickets through SISTIC ℮ www.singapore dancetheatre.com
Ⓜ Dhoby Ghaut ♿

Ho, Ho, X'Ho

Even the most draconian of medieval courts boasted a court jester. In Singapore this mischievous role falls to punk rocker, writer, DJ, cultural jammer, professional whiner and self-appointed Wake-Up Call, X'Ho. X'Ho, who has been published in *Big O* music magazine and, funnily enough, conservative *The Straits Times*, is one of the few public voices of dissent. Favourite peeves range from rants against censorship and cutting social critique to self-indulgent moans about slow-mo pedestrians.

Singapore Symphony Orchestra (3, K6)

This orchestra plays weekly at the Victoria Concert Hall. In addition to classical favourites, it jazzes things up a little with free concerts in the Botanic Gardens, Young People's Concerts (fusing multimedia, puppetry and theatre) and SSO Casual Concerts with tea and Q&A sessions thrown in. Book in advance – no children under the age of four.

✉ Victoria Concert Hall, 11 Empress Pl ☎ book through SISTIC ℮ www.sso.org.sg
Ⓜ Raffles Place ☺ most sessions 8.15pm ⓢ $11-120 depending on event; student & senior citizen (60+) discounts are available

Traditional Beijing opera at the Chinese Theatre Circle.

THEATRE & COMEDY

Singapore boasts a happening theatre scene. Check the daily and street press for details. See also Esplanade – Theatres on the Bay, pp. 20-1.

Action Theatre

(3, F6) This non-profit company produces original works about contemporary themes. Its play *Mail Order Brides and other Oriental Takeaways* was the first Singaporean play to be produced in New York.
✉ 42 Waterloo St
☎ 6837 0842
e www.action.org.sg
Ⓜ City Hall

Boom Boom Room

(3, L5) Before relocating, this cabaret club was once an institution of the notorious Bugis St. There are home-grown comedy /cabaret shows nightly, but the weekend draw-card remains veteran drag queen Kumar's dance and lip-sync act to everything from Canto pop to Hindustani. Keep a low profile – the humour can get personal.
✉ Far East Sq, 130-32 Amoy St ☎ 6435 0030
Ⓜ Raffles Place
🕐 shows start from 10pm ⑤ $10-25

Guinness Theatre

(3, H5) This experimental arts complex features a small theatre promoting local works by young and emerging Singaporean artists. To keep things accessible and interesting tickets are free, low-priced or 'pay what you think it's worth'.
✉ Substation, 45 Armenian St ☎ 6337 7800 e www.substation.org Ⓜ City Hall
🕐 box office Mon-Fri 4-8.30pm ♿

Livid Room Productions

This award-winning company was founded by a couple of 21-year-old actresses. Their recent production, *Stop Kiss*, about lesbian love, suggests that Singapore's first feminist theatre group isn't messing around. Go girl!
✉ various venues
e lividroom@hotmail.com, www.muttflush.com/stopkiss/

The Necessary Stage

(5, D6) One of Singapore's best-known experimental theatre groups, its penchant for dark, wrist-slashing works can make it the target of local jokes. It does some great, interactive and collaborative works with schools.
✉ #B1-02 Marine Pde Community Bldg, 278 Marine Pde Rd ☎ 6440 8115 e www.necessary.org 🚌 16, 76, 197
⑤ approx $21-35 ♿

Singapore Repertory Theatre (3, J3)

This company is the bigwig of Singapore's theatre scene; expect to see repertory standards like *The Glass Menagerie*, *Hamlet* and *Death of a Salesman* plus original works.
✉ DBS Drama Centre, 20 Merbau Rd ☎ 6733 8166 e www.singrep.com 🚌 65, 139, 970

Theatreworks (3, G5)

This contemporary company produces local works with local actors – a good chance to see what's going on in Singapore's drama scene. Recent works include *Machine* – a play about contemporary love affairs and a washing machine.
✉ The Black Box, Cox Terrace ☎ 6338 4077, tickets through SISTIC e www.theatreworks.org.sg
Ⓜ Dhoby Ghaut ♿

Toy Factory Ensemble (3, M4)

This contemporary bilingual theatre company is going from strength to strength; pushing the boundaries and producing a strong range of international and local works. Recent productions include Britain's *Beautiful Thing*, a gay love story transported from a British housing estate setting to a Singaporean HDB block; *Shopping and F***ing*; and Ibsen's *A Doll House*.
✉ 15A Smith St
☎ 6221 1526 e www.toyfactory.org
Ⓜ Outram Park

Wild Rice

Singapore's sexiest theatre company was founded by Ivan Heng, famous for his drag interpretation of *Emily of Emerald Hill* (see p. 70), and boasts Glen Goei, who directed the Singaporean favourite *Forever Fever*, as associate artistic director.
✉ various venues
☎ 6223 9081 e www.wildrice.com.sg

CINEMAS

Singapore has one of the world's highest cinema-going populations. Most films shown in Singapore are Hollywood blockbusters; the rest are mostly mainstream European or art-house films, Hong Kong action films and Bollywood musicals. Non-English films are usually subtitled. Weekend sessions, even midnight sessions, sell out so book ahead and be prepared to queue. Check *The Straits Times* for session details. It's not uncommon for people to chat incessantly and receive mobile phone calls during films.

Alliance Française

(3, A2) The Alliance Française shows classic and contemporary French films every Tuesday night at 9pm unless listed otherwise on its website – you can also enjoy a glass of wine in the on-site cafe.

✉ 1 Sarkies Rd
☎ 6737 8422 (Mon-Fri 9am-7.30pm, Sat 9am-4pm) e www.alliance francaise.org.sg
Ⓜ Newton Ⓢ $8

GV Gold Class (3, H1)

Singapore's swishest cinema offers lush carpeting, single and double reclining seats complete with footrests, table service and a reasonable menu. Recommended for romance and self-pampering.

✉ #03-39/40 Great World City, 1 Kim Seng Promenade ☎ 6735 8484 (11am-9pm)

e www.goldenvillage .com.sg 🚌 75, 195, 970 Ⓢ $25 (ticket only)

Lido (4, B4)

All the big Hollywood blockbusters and mainstream releases are shown here at the conveniently located Shaw House.

✉ L5, Shaw House, 350 Orchard Rd
☎ 6732 4124, credit card bookings 6738 0555 e www.shaw .com.sg Ⓜ Orchard ♿

OMNI Theatre (2, F5)

Omni shows 3D films (about space, dolphins, nature etc) and Walt Disney blockbusters projected onto a 23m hemispheric screen. It also offers 18-seater 'Virtual Voyage' simulation rides.

✉ 15 Science Centre Rd ☎ 6425 2500
e www.sci-ctr.edu.sg
🚌 335 from Ⓜ Jurong

East ⏰ 10am to last show 8pm
Ⓢ Omnitheatre: $10/5, Virtual Voyage: $6/4
♿ must be over 90cm for Virtual Voyage

Overseas Movie: Golden (3, E10)

Here you might find the odd German art-house flick showing alongside a Korean melodrama or Chinese ghost story.

✉ #03-00 Golden Mile Tower, 6001 Beach Rd
☎ 6298 5466
e www.oegroup.com .sg Ⓜ Lavender ♿

Shaw Complex: Prince & Jade

(3, G8) Seating 1200 and with an enormous screen this is Singapore's largest cinema.

✉ Shaw Tower, 100 Beach Rd ☎ 6391 2550, credit card bookings 6738 0555
e www.shaw.com.sg
Ⓜ Raffles Place ♿

Singapore International Film Festival

Film buffs should check out the festival (around April). Expect a good range of international films plus new home-grown films unlikely to be seen elsewhere.

✉ various cinemas
e www.filmfest .org.sg ♿

One for the ladies: movie-poster promises.

places to stay

While Orchard Rd groans with high-end massive hotel chains you can find smaller, boutique-style mid-range hotels around the Chinatown and Little India districts. The Singaporean government isn't a big fans of backpackers – it recently razed the entire budget hotel strip along Bencoolen St for 'redevelopment'. (Another shopping mall perhaps?) Consequently penny-pinching pickings are slim and those remaining are pretty grim.

Room Rates

Hotels are grouped according to published rates for a standard double room.

Deluxe	$400-650
Top End	$200-399
Mid-Range	$100-199
Budget	$40-99

As usual, top-end hotels supply top-end facilities for top-end prices: expect great service, fitness centres, swimming pools and business facilities. Note that not all mid-range and budget rooms have windows, especially in older buildings; however, all hotels have air-con options and most have lifts. Smaller, independent hotels tend to have a more interesting vibe than the corporate monsters.

In the major hotels, a 3% goods and services tax (GST), 1% government tax and 10% service charge are added to your bill. This is the 'plus-plus-plus' that follows the quoted price (eg, $140+++), while 'nett' means that the price includes tax and service charge. The hotels stipulate that you should not tip when a service charge applies. GST and government taxes also apply to the cheaper hotels but are usually included in the quoted price. Prices are usually quoted in Singapore dollars.

Singapore's hotel industry is extremely competitive and even top-end hotels offer frequent special promotions and substantial discounts for longer stays, repeat visits or corporate rates, so it's worth asking. Also, paying a little bit more can often yield a worthwhile upgrade. Following the post–11 September 2001 tourism slump some top-end hotels were offering rooms at almost half their published rates.

Cross the threshold into a world of fine hotels on Orchard Rd (no rollerskates allowed).

DELUXE

Four Seasons (4, C3)
This excellent hotel boasts European-style furnishings with Asiatic touches including an interesting art collection. With air-conditioned tennis courts, an excellent fitness centre and two swimming pools this hotel caters to the fitness freak while the excellent restaurants will please the gourmets.
✉ 190 Orchard Blvd
☎ 6831 7300; fax 6733 0669 e www.fshr.com
Ⓜ Orchard ♿

The Fullerton (3, K7)
Since this 1928 building was restored as a hotel it has fast become one of *the* places to stay in Singapore. Offering elegant, luxurious, modern surroundings the hotel has a great riverside location near to some of Singapore's best tourist and nightlife attractions.
✉ 1 Fullerton Sq
☎ 6733 3833; fax 6733 8388 e www.fullerton hotel.com
Ⓜ Raffles Place

Goodwood Park Hotel (4, A5)
Dating from the 1900s this Germanic-inspired building features an unbelievably twee fountain and wall-to-wall pastel pink in the lobby. The rooms however, are terrific with modern but cosy furnishings and plenty of windows and room to move. The hotel has a pleasant, green poolside area, friendly staff and good corporate rates.
✉ 22 Scotts Rd
☎ 6737 7411; fax 6732 8558
e www.good woodparkhotel.com.sg
Ⓜ Orchard ♿

Grand Hyatt (4, B5)
The lush garden, pool, fitness centre, and recreation facilities, popular restaurant, central location and luxurious and spacious rooms make this a favourite spot for corporate guests. Executive-class rooms boast bonus private Balinese-style gardens.
✉ 10-12 Scotts Rd
☎ 6738 1234; fax 6732 1696 e www .singapore.hyatt.com
Ⓜ Orchard ♿

Inter-Continental (3, F7) Reputed to be one of the best hotels in South-East Asia, the beautifully restored Inter-Continental is housed in an extended and restored set of shopfronts midway between the colonial area and Arab St. Expect great service and overall sumptuousness. The gym and pool are great.
✉ 80 Middle Rd
☎ 6338 7600;

Sentosa Island

There is a range of accommodation available on Sentosa Island (p. 30), from top-end five-star comfort at **Shangri-La's Rasa Sentosa resort** (1, B2; ☎ 6275 0100; fax 6275 0335; e www.shangri-la.com), to the mid-range **Beaufort Hotel** (1, D5; ☎ 6275 0331; fax 6275 0228; e www.beaufort.com.sg) and **Sijori Resort** (1, C3; ☎ 6271 2002; fax 6274 0220; e wwwx.sijoriresort.com.sg).

Chalet resort accommodation is available at the **NTUC Sentosa Beach Resort** (1, B3; ☎ 6275 1034; fax 6275 1074). For budget options there's the basic **Sentosa Holiday Chalets** (1, D5), the **Sentosa Youth Hostel** (1, D4) – although given the development next door it's unlikely to be quiet – and **Camp Laguna** at Central Beach (1, D4) – tents can be hired for $15-20. For information call ☎ 6270 7888 (9am-5pm), fax 6270 7888, e accommodation@sentosa.com.sg; www.sentosa.com.sg.

Stay on Sentosa for some laid-back sun and fun.

fax 6338 7366
e www.interconti.com
M Bugis

Meritus Negara
(4, B3) You almost need a torch to navigate the solid black granite of the lobby. The 200 rooms feature black lacquer and gold Oriental furnishings and a soft grey colour scheme; bold and dramatic yet a little austere. Deluxe rooms are reasonably spacious but the Superior rooms are poky. No charge for children under 12 staying in parents' room (max 2).
✉ 10 Claymore Rd
☎ 6737 0811; fax 6737 9075 **e** negara@
meritus-hotels.com;
www.meritus-negara
.com.sg **M** Orchard ♿

Raffles (3, H7)
Is it worth coughing up to stay at Raffles? Well, despite a written application for a hotel tour we didn't get a guernsey, so all we can say is either Raffles is very, very busy or it's simply not concerned about increasing its publicity. Still, there's only one Raffles. Regular rooms

Gay Stays
Checking into hotels in a straight nation can be tedious. The **Tropical Hotel** (p. 108) and the **Hotel 81** chain (**e** hotel@hotel81.com.sg; www.hotel81.com .sg) are both gay-friendly, but they're hardly deluxe. Given that the queer community congregates around Chinatown you may find hotels in this area more receptive, or at least more accustomed to same-sex couples. Alternatively, large hotel chains provide greater anonymity than small, family-run businesses.

cost $650-950, suites from $3000.
✉ 1 Beach Rd **☎** 6337 1886; fax 6339 7650
e raffles@raffles.com;
www.raffles.com
M City Hall

Shangri-La Hotel
(4, A1) After the golden opulence of the lobby the rooms in this award-winning hotel feel a little tired, with dated furnishings and slightly squishy spaces. However, the landscaped gardens are beautiful and the service excellent. There's a 24hr business centre.
✉ 22 Orange Grove Rd
☎ 6737 3644; fax 6737 3257 **e** sls@shangri-la

.com; www.shangri-la
.com **M** Orchard ♿

Sheraton Towers
(3, B1) The decor is a little stiff but the Sheraton is definitely one of the city's most appealing hotels. Rooms are comfortable and large with good views and all room categories enjoy full butler service. The lobby restaurant features a waterfall picture window and the lively staff are eager to please.
✉ 39 Scotts Rd
☎ 6737 6888; fax 6737 1072 **e** sheraton.tow ers.singapore@shera ton.com; www.shera ton.com **M** Newton ♿

Quench your thirst in style at Raffles.

TOP END

Hilton (4, C3)

The standard rooms in this corporate-style hotel are not overly spacious, however business travellers staying on the Executive Floor will enjoy a complimentary breakfast, all-day snacks and beverages, a suit pressing and use of the fitness centre. The rooftop pool is rather small.

✉ 581 Orchard Rd
☎ 6737 2233; fax 6732 2917 ⓔ hitels@pacific .net.sg; www.singapore .hilton.com Ⓜ Orchard

Le Meridien (4, C10)

Airline crew clutter up the soaring glass lobby with see-through capsule lifts. Rooms are bright and tasteful but attempts at 'homey touches' lose out to an overall corporate vibe. Poolside rooms have balconies.

✉ 100 Orchard Rd
☎ 6733 8855; fax 6732 7886 ⓔ meridien -resvn@pacific.net; www.lemeridien -singapore.com Ⓜ Dhoby Ghaut

Marriott (4, B5)

The distinctive Marriott Hotel (the tall, angular one with a funny Asian 'hat') offers a good business centre and tasteful, cosy rooms which, despite the five-star hotel ambience, manage to feel quite homey.

✉ 320 Orchard Rd
☎ 6735 5800; fax 6735 9800 ⓔ www.marriott .com Ⓜ Orchard ♿

Pan Pacific (3, J8)

This 800-room hotel is quite a popular spot with business travellers so you can expect a corporate feel. However, a recent refurb aimed at Gen-X execs gave the 33rd and 34th floors a much more contemporary look with funky colours and groovy furnishings. Pump iron at the good Clark Hatch gym on-site.

✉ 7 Raffles Blvd
☎ 6336 8111; fax 6339 1861 ⓔ www.panpac .com Ⓜ Raffles City

Swissôtel (3, H7)

Everyone is raving about the rebranded 2000-room Swissôtel (formerly the Westin Stamford). Designed by IM Pei, the hotel boasts fabulous views (it's the tallest hotel in South-East Asia) and one of Singapore's hippest wining and dining complexes.

✉ 2 Stamford Rd
☎ 6338 8585; fax 6338 2862 ⓔ www.raffles .com Ⓜ City Hall

Serviced Apartments

For long-term accommodation the five-star **Le Grove Serviced Apartments** (32 Orange Grove Rd; 4, A1; ☎ 6732 2212; fax 6738 9281; ⓔ legrove@ cdl.com.sg), just near the Shangri-La Hotel, features daily housekeeping, weekday breakfast and good facilities. Alternatively try **Singapore Homefinders** (ⓔ homefinders@apeclink.com; www.apeclink.com /homefinders), which has a range of short- and longer-term accommodation options with and without housekeeping services.

Moving through the Marriott.

MID-RANGE

Bencoolen (3, F6)
It's nothing to knot your knickers over, but the location is good, the rooms are serviceable, the bathrooms OK and it's one of the few hotels in this price range to offer a swimming pool (although admittedly it's more suited to get-wet-dips than actual movement).
✉ **47 Bencoolen St** ☎ **6336 0822; fax 6336 2250** e **bencoolen@ pacific.net.sg** Ⓜ **Dhoby Ghaut**

Damenlou Hotel
(3, M4) This hotel offers reasonably spacious, comfortable rooms with some Chinese furnishings and old-fashioned shutter windows, in a quiet spot in one of the most happening parts of town. The owner is friendly, rates are negotiable and the rooftop cafe offers quirky views onto Chinatown.
✉ **12 Ann Siang Rd** ☎ **6221 1900; fax 6225 8500** Ⓜ **Outram Park** ♿

The Duxton (Berjaya Hotel) (3, N3)
This beautifully restored boutique hotel in the heart of Chinatown offers plush, elegant rooms in an interesting location. Rooms overlooking the street have views, but standard rooms do not. Suites are over two floors. There's no swimming pool or gym but the atmosphere compensates.
✉ **83 Duxton Rd** ☎ **6227 7678; fax 6227 1232** e **duxton@ singnet.com.sg; www .singaporehotels.net/dux ton** Ⓜ **Tanjong Pagar**

Gallery Hotel (3, J2)
Singapore's only 'hip hotel' boasts Philippe Starck fittings, a glass rooftop swimming pool, art gallery, great restaurant and nightlife options and free internet access on I-Macs. Rooms feature retro furnishings in bright colours and even standard category rooms are spacious, however the Bookend Club room layout is awkward.
✉ **76 Robertson Quay** ☎ **6849 8686; fax 6836 6666** e **general@ galleryhotel.com.sg** 🚌 **65, 139, 970**

The Inn at Temple Street (3, L4)
This place is popular with tour groups, suggesting that while not remarkable, or even especially charming, it is at least clean and reliable. It offers a great location in Chinatown and reasonable rates.
✉ **36 Temple St** ☎ **6221 5333; fax 6225 5391** e **www.theinn .com.sg** Ⓜ **Outram Park** ♿

Orchard Hotel (4, B2)
Friendly management lends a personal touch to this 600-room hotel. The Claymore Wing has been recently revamped and rooms feature blonde woods, earthy tones and white linen. Elsewhere a slightly dowdy brown and beige colour scheme reigns. Rooms smell strongly of cleaning products, but the place offers good promotions.
✉ **442 Orchard Rd** ☎ **6734 7766; fax 6733 5482** e **enquiry@ orchardhotel.com.sg; www.orchardhotel.com .sg** Ⓜ **Orchard** ♿

Regalis Court (4, E9)
Just around the corner from Killiney and Orchard Rds, this historic hotel offers charmingly furnished and family-friendly spacious rooms – even the smallest seem more cute than poky. Standard rooms don't have windows but they do have good-sized bathrooms.
✉ **64 Lloyd Rd** ☎ **6734 7117; fax 6736 1651** e **regalis court@pacific.net.sg; www.regalis.com.sg** Ⓜ **Somerset** ♿

The Royal Peacock
(3, M3) This small hotel in a restored shophouse falls short of the nearby Duxton's standards, but the prices are sometimes slashed to budget level. Standard rooms lack windows and none are particularly spacious, however it has more character than a standard hotel and the location is vibrant.
✉ **55 Keong Saik Rd** ☎ **6223 3522; fax 6221 1770** e **rpeacock@ cyberway.com.sg** Ⓜ **Outram Park**

Hold court at the Regalis.

BUDGET

Classique Hotel (3, C8)
With window rooms offered at $65 ($80 for up to three people) this place must be one of the best deals in Singapore. It boasts friendly staff, good-sized rooms with floor to ceiling windows and nicely appointed bathrooms with full-sized bath. The modern cafe downstairs is a little cold, but Klimt prints in the rooms somehow seem nice rather than cheesy.
✉ **240 Jalan Besar**
☎ **6392 3838; fax 6392 2828** Ⓜ **Lavender** ⚥

Dickson Court Hotel
(3, D7) This place claims to be 'boutique' but rooms are small and dark, and the hotel has an off-the-rack kind of feel. It's OK but nothing to write home about.
✉ **3 Dickson Rd**
☎ **6297 7811; fax 6297 7833** ℮ **dickson1@ magix.com.sg** 🚌 **106, 111, 147**

The Keong Saik Hotel (3, M3)
In a renovated shophouse in Chinatown, standard rooms at this vaguely charming hotel do not have windows and even deluxe rooms are tiny, not to mention the bathrooms. Rooms feature wooden floorboards and tasteful but spartan Asian furnishings – mainly a bed.
✉ **69 Keong Saik Rd**
☎ **6225 0660; fax 6225 0660** ℮ **keongsaik@ pacific.net.sg**
Ⓜ **Outram Park**

Kerbau Hotel (3, D6)
Housed in an old-style building, the downstairs rooms are windowless, but some upstairs rooms have interesting views onto Kerbau Rd –

though these could be noisy. The rooms are fairly shabby but you can expect to knock off $10 from published rates.
✉ **54/62 Kerbau Rd**
☎ **6297 6668; fax 6297 6669** 🚌 **65, 97, 103**

Lloyd's Inn (4, E10)
Strangely interesting 1940s-style building with ill-advised dark, period wallpaper and odd, angular rooms which range from the dark and depressing to small but bright with pretty garden views. It's in an interesting location near crumbling mansions, Killiney and Orchard Rds. Book double beds in advance.
✉ **2 Lloyd Rd**
☎ **6737 7309; fax 6737 7847** ℮ **mail@lloydinn .com;www.lloydinn .com** Ⓜ **Somerset** ⚥

Perak Lodge (3, D7)
With all the guidebook writers cluttering up the lobby you'd almost have to be lucky to get a room at this cosy, restored hotel in the heart of Little India. Typically, standard rooms are small and without windows but other categories are bright and roomy enough. Staff are friendly and helpful with inquiries.
✉ **12 Perak Rd**
☎ **6299 7733; fax 6392 0919** ℮ **perlodge@ singnet.com.sg; www .peraklodge.net**
Ⓜ **Bugis** ⚥

Sloane Court Hotel
(3, A1) This kitsch, mock-Tudor lodge is somehow endearing. Not all the rooms have windows, but polished floorboards, brightly renovated bathrooms, English-style furnishings and friendly staff

lend it a quirky appeal.
✉ **17 Balmoral Rd**
☎ **6235 3311 fax 6733 9041** ℮ **sloane@sing net.com.sg** 🚌 **603, 66**

South East Asia Hotel (3, F7)
OK, it's nothing flash, but this friendly little hotel offers reasonably sized, clean rooms, some with views to the plaza below. Next door is one of Singapore's busiest temples.
✉ **190 Waterloo St**
☎ **6338 2394; fax 6338 3480** ℮ **seahotel@ singnet.com.sg; www .seahotel.com.sg**
Ⓜ **Bugis**

Tropical Hotel (3, M3)
Compared to its deluxe neighbours the slightly seedy Tropical Hotel is a little worse for wear, suggesting the clientele may not be there for the decor. It is, however, very gay friendly.
✉ **22 Teck Lim Rd**
☎ **6225 6696; fax 6225 6626** Ⓜ **Outram Park**

YMCA Metropolitan
(4, A4) Popular with missionaries and student groups, the YMCA (20min walk to Orchard Rd) offers small, clean, safe but dowdy rooms with pool and laundry access. Standard rooms are windowless and there's no dormitory; families will probably find better deals elsewhere. (YMCA's International House branch in Orchard Rd can be contacted on ☎ 6430 2304.)
✉ **60 Stevens Rd**
☎ **6737 7755; fax 6235 5528** ℮ **hotel@mymca .org.sg; www.mymca .org.sg** 🚌 **190, 605, 105, 132** ⚥

facts for the visitor

The beautiful blue-tiled Malabar Muslim Jama-Ath Mosque.

ARRIVAL & DEPARTURE

Singapore is a business and travel hub and its airport receives an incredible amount of air traffic. You should have no problems securing reasonably priced and direct flights.

Air

Singapore's slick and squeaky-clean Changi airport (2, E14) is about 20km east of the city centre. It has two terminals with a third under construction. Most airlines operate from Terminal 1; the following operate from Terminal 2: Air Canada, Air France, Royal Brunei Airlines, Lufthansa, Malaysia Airlines, SilkAir, Air New Zealand, Philippine Airlines, Singapore Airlines and Virgin Atlantic Airways. Facilities at Changi include: 24hr medical centre (basement of Terminal 2), free phones for local calls, free Internet access between 11pm and 6am at the E-Hub (Terminal 2), and a children's playground; for details consult the information brochures distributed throughout the airport.

Changi International Airport
Left Luggage

Rates for left luggage range from $1 to $9 depending on the item's size. See the counter in Basement 2 for details.

Information

General Inquiries
☎ 6541 2267

Lost Property
☎ 1800 541 2107/8

Flight Information
☎ 1800 542 4422

Hotel Booking Service
☎ 6542 6966 (Terminal 1)
☎ 6545 9789 (Terminal 2)

Airport Access

The train is the best way to reach the city. Trains leave Changi airport every 12mins from 5.30am to 11.18pm. The fare is around $1.40. If you catch the train from the city to the airport you may have to change at Tanah Merah station. Trains to the airport operate from City Hall approx 6am to midnight.

Buses leave for the city from Terminal 1 (Basement 2) and Terminal 2 (Basement). The trip takes 1hr and costs around $1.50, you must have the exact change. Bus No 36 goes directly to Orchard Rd.

Shuttle buses to the CBD and most hotels leave every 30mins from 6am to 6pm and every 15mins from 6.05pm to midnight. They cost $7/5. Book at the counter in the arrivals hall and pay the driver.

Taxis to the city cost around $20 plus surcharges: $5 Fri-Sun 5pm to midnight, midnight to 6am the surcharge is 50% of the total fare; it's $3 at all other times.

Bus

Air-conditioned express buses leave daily for neighbouring Malaysia and Thailand. Buses to Thailand usually depart from the Gold Mile Complex (3, 10E) on Beach Rd while buses to Malaysia leave from the bus terminal on the corner of Lavender St and Kallang Bahru (3, B9; opposite the Kallang Bahru Complex).

Contact these numbers directly for details, or approach a Singapore Tourist Bureau (STB) office for assistance:

Singapore – Johor Bahru	☎ 6292 8146
Singapore – Kuala Lumpur	☎ 6292 8254
Singapore – Malacca	☎ 6293 5915
Singapore – Thailand	☎ 6293 6692

Train

From Singapore there are three air-conditioned express trains daily to Malaysia (approx 6hrs to Kuala Lumpur) and daily trains to Thailand (via Butterworth in Malaysia). For information see @ www.ktmb.com.my or contact Malayan Railway on ☎ 6222 5165. Depending on the carriage class and whether you ride in a seat or a sleeper, fares are approximately $20-70 to Kuala Lumpur, $40-135 to Butterworth and $65-100 to Thailand.

The luxury Eastern & Oriental Express travels from Singapore to Bangkok, Chiang Mai, Kuala Lumpur, Angkor Wat and Butterworth. Fares are $1,200-5000. For details see @ www.orient-express.com or contact E&O (☎ 6392 3500).

Boat

Ferry services depart daily from the World Trade Centre (1, A4) and Tanah Merah (2, F14) ferry terminals and ply routes between Singapore and neighbouring islands of Indonesia and Malaysia. Fares range from $27/17 return to Batam Island (Indonesia) to $148/93 to Tioman Island (Malaysia). Some services may not operate during the monsoon season (late Oct-Mar). Each destination has its own ferry operators – ask the STB for contact details.

Travel Documents

Passports & Visas

At the time of publication travellers from the USA, UK, Australia, NZ, Canada and South Africa receive an automatic 30-day tourist visa on entry. Passports must be valid for six months and you need a return plane ticket and evidence of sufficient funds for your stay. Women more than six months pregnant must make a special application to their nearest Singaporean embassy. To extend a visa contact Singapore Immigration and Registration (10 Kallang Rd; ☎ 6391 6100). Applications take at least one day to process.

Customs

No drugs (don't even think about it), guns, firecrackers, obscene publications or chewing gum are allowed. Take a letter from your doctor if you carry prescription medication. Bring as much cash as you like.

Duty Free

Visitors to Singapore are allowed to bring in 1L of wine, beer or spirits duty free providing they are over 18 years old, have not arrived from Malaysia and have been away from Singapore for at least 48hrs.

Departure Tax

Singapore charges $15 departure tax (subject to change); the cost is included in your ticket price.

GETTING AROUND

Singapore has excellent public transport with bus and train routes covering most areas of interest. The train is the easiest system to navigate but you may find stops a little far apart – walking in 35°C for any distance is hard work. Expansion of the system is underway. Due to limitations on car ownership taxis are also considered public transport. For an overview of the Mass Rapid Transit (MRT) and bus system buy the handy pocket-sized *TransitLink Guide* ($1.50), available from MRT ticket sales offices and bookshops.

Travel Passes

You can purchase unlimited-travel Singapore Explorer all-day/three-day tickets for $5/12 at major hotels and MRT stations. They are valid only for the date printed on the ticket – ask for an alternative date to be printed if you wish to purchase one in advance. They are valid for one person only. Alternatively buy a Transitlink Farecard ticket. You can purchase Farecards from MRT stations and 7-Eleven stores for $2 plus $10 worth of travel. You can top them up at stations or ATM-style machines at stations – however the machines may not take credit cards. You can refund any unused credit at major MRT stations.

Bus

Buses run between 6am and midnight, leave every few minutes and go almost anywhere. Timetables (available on board) and some bus stops list the major landmarks for particular bus routes. Bus fares are 70c to $1.50. There are also a few flat-rate buses. You must have the exact fare as no change is given. Alternatively use a Farecard (see Travel Passes, above). For inquiries see e www.sbstransit.com.sg or call ☎ 1800 287 9366. For lost property call ☎ 6383 7211.

Tourist Buses

Singapore airlines runs the SIA Hop-On tourist bus which loops around the main tourist areas. It operates daily (every 30mins) 8.30am-7pm. Tickets are available from the driver and cost $6/4 for a day pass, or $3

with a Singapore Airlines or SilkAir boarding pass or ticket.

The Singapore Trolley is a tourist bus not-so-cunningly disguised as an old-fashioned tram. It also circuits the major tourist sites. It operates 9.40am-4.55pm and costs around $15/10, which includes a riverboat ride from Clarke Quay. Purchase tickets from the driver.

Train

The ultra-clean and efficient MRT subway system is the most comfortable and hassle-free way to navigate Singapore. The trains run from around 5.30am to midnight and depart every 3-4mins (peak times) and every 6-8mins (off-peak). Fares start at 80c. Consult the *TransitLink Guide* ($1.50) for routes, call ☎ 1800 336 8900 or check out e www.smrtcorp.com.

Taxi

Taxis are plentiful in Singapore except at 'changing shift' between 10pm and 11pm when it can be impossible to find one. Taxis are metered and cost around $2.10 for the first kilometre, then 10c for each additional 240m. The average journey costs $5-10. A list of fares and surcharges is displayed in each cab. Surcharges are levied for telephone ($3) and advance ($6) bookings. There's a surcharge of $3 for each journey *from* the airport but not *to*, a $1.50 surcharge on all trips from the CBD between 4.30 and 7pm on weekdays and from 11.30am to 2pm Saturdays. You may also have to pay a surcharge if you take the taxi into the CBD during restricted hours (see Car & Motorcycle, p. 112). If you pay by credit card, you are charged an extra 10%. To catch a taxi, flag one off the street or find a taxi stand at a major hotel or shopping plaza.

If you order a taxi by phone you'll be asked your name and destination; a message then tells you the registration of your cab. Taxi companies include:

City Cab	
cash bookings	☎ 6552 2222
credit card bookings	☎ 6553 8888
Comfort CabLink	☎ 6552 1111
TIBS	☎ 6555 8888

Car & Motorcycle

Unsurprisingly traffic in Singapore is fairly orderly, but the profusion of one-way streets and streets that change names (sometimes several times) plus restricted zones and the parking system can make driving complicated for the uninitiated. Given Singapore's superb public transport and cheap taxis it's unlikely that you'll need to drive, but if you do, get a copy of the *Singapore Street Directory* and take note: from 7.30am-6.30pm weekdays, and from 10.15am-2pm Saturdays, the area encompassing the CBD, Chinatown and Orchard Rd is a restricted zone. Cars are charged a toll for entry by sensors on overhanging gantries. The sensors prompt drivers to insert a cash card into their in-vehicle unit, which then extracts the toll. The same system also operates on certain major highways. Rental cars are subject to the same regulations. Cameras on the gantries automatically photograph cars that don't pay the entry toll and a fine is sent to the car owner's address.

Parking in many places in Singapore operates on a coupon system. You can buy a booklet of coupons at parking kiosks and post offices. You must display a coupon in your car window with holes punched out to indicate the time, day and date your car was parked.

Road Rules

Singaporeans drive on the left side of the road and it is compulsory to wear seat belts. The legal driving age in Singapore is 18-60. Anyone over 60 must have a medical check.

City speed limit is 50km/h in residential areas and 80-90km/h on freeways. Speed cameras operate throughout Singapore. You may not drive if your blood alcohol concentration exceeds 80mg per 100mL of blood.

Rental

For local driving many of the smaller operators quote slightly cheaper rates than the major companies. Rental rates are more expensive than in Malaysia, and there are surcharges for taking a Singaporean rental car onto the mainland. If you intend renting a car to drive in Malaysia, it is much better to rent in Johor Bahru.

Rates start from $160 a day but weekly rates are cheaper. Some companies may demand that drivers are aged over 23. Special deals may be available, especially for longer-term rental. There are hire booths at Changi airport and in the city. Some of the main operators are:

Avis	☎ 6737 1668
Budget Rent a Car	☎ 6742 0119
Hertz Rent-a-Car	☎ 6734 4646

Driving Licence & Permit

Your home-country licence is all you need for the first six months.

Motoring Organisations

If you hire a car ensure that you are entitled to Automobile Association assistance. Helpful contacts include:

Automobile Association of Singapore (AAS)	☎ 6737 2444
AAS 24hr Emergency Road Service	☎ 6748 9911
Traffic Police	☎ 6547 0000

PRACTICAL INFORMATION

Climate & When to Go

Nov-Jan is the wettest time, however temperature and rainfall are steady year-round. You might like your trip to coincide with one of Singapore's many festivals; Chinese New Year (January/February), Festival of the Hungry Ghosts (August/September) and Thaipusam (January) are among the most spectacular. Alternatively, the Singapore Food Festival and the Great Singapore Sale are held in July.

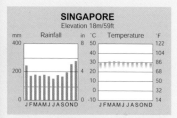

Tourist Information

Tourist Information Abroad

The Singapore Tourist Bureau (STB) has various offices abroad including:

Australia
L11, AWA Bldg, 47 York St, Sydney, NSW 2000 (☎ 02-9290 2888, fax 9290 2555; [e] stb-syd@stb-syd.org.au)

Canada
Suite 404, 2 Bloor St W, Toronto, Ontario M4W 3E2 (☎ 416-363 8898, fax 363 5752; [e] AskMich@TourismSingapore .com)

New Zealand
Marketing Representative c-/Vivaldi World Limited, 85B Hebron Rd, Waiake, Auckland 1311 (☎ 09-473 8658; [e] stb.Auckland@xtra.co.nz)

UK
1st floor, Carrington House, 126-130 Regent St, London W1R 5FE (☎ 020-7437 0033, fax 7734 2191; [e] info@stb.org.uk)

USA
[e] www.tourismsingapore.com
Chicago: Suite 2615 Two Prudential Plaza, 180 North Stetson Ave, Chicago IL 60601 (☎ 312-938 1888, fax 938 0086)
Los Angeles: Suite 501 4929 Wilshire Blvd, Los Angeles CA 900010 (☎ 323-677 0808, fax 677 0801; [e] AskVince@ TourismSingapore.com)
New York: 12th fl, 590 Fifth Ave, New York, NY 10036 (☎ 212-302 4861, fax 302 4801; [e] AskRoc@TourismSingapore.com)

Local Tourist Information

The STB head office is on Orchard Spring Lane, but the office at Suntec City provides a wider range of services including tour bookings and event ticketing. Its website is [e] www.newasia-singapore.com. The STB also runs a tourist information hotline (☎ 1800 736 2000).

Singapore Visitors Centre @ Liang Court
#01-35/41 Liang Court Shopping Centre, 177 River Valley Rd (3, J4; ☎ 6336 2888; open 10.30am-9.30pm)

Singapore Visitors Centre @ Suntec City
#01-35/37/39/41 Suntec City, 3 Temasek Blvd (3, H8; ☎ 1800 332 5066; open 8am-6.30pm)

Singapore Visitors Centre @ Tourism Court
1 Orchard Spring Lane (4, E1; ☎ 1 800 736 2000; open Mon-Fri 8.30am-5pm, to 1pm Saturday)

Singapore Visitors Centre @ Chijmes
#01-20 Chijmes, 30 Victoria St. (3, H6; ☎ 6338 2529; open Mon-Sat 10am-6pm)

Embassies & Consulates

Many foreign consulates and embassies are conveniently located in the Orchard Rd area (Map 4).

Addresses for some of them include:

Australia
25 Napier Rd (2, G8; ☎ 6836 4100, fax 6737 5481; e sing@dfat.gov.au)

Canada
#14-00 IBM Towers, 80 Anson Rd (3,P4; ☎ 6325 3200, fax 6325 3297)

New Zealand
#15-06 Ngee Ann City, Tower A, 391A Orchard Rd (4, C6; ☎ 6235 9966, fax 6733 9924)

South Africa
#15-01/06 Ordeon Towers, 331 North Bridge Rd (3, G7; ☎ 6339 6658)

UK
100 Tanglin Rd (2, G8; ☎ 6473 9333, fax 6475 9706)

USA
27 Napier Rd (2, G8; ☎ 6476 9100, fax 6476 9340; e www.usembassy singapore.org.sg)

Money

Currency
The unit of currency is the Singaporean dollar. Singapore uses 1c, 5c, 10c, 20c, 50c and $1 coins, while notes come in denominations of $2, $5, $10, $50, $100, $500 and $1000; Singapore also has a $10,000 note – not that you'll see many. The Singaporean dollar is made up of 100 cents.

Travellers Cheques
Travellers cheques are good for backup when all else fails. They can be purchased at post offices in Singapore and can sometimes be used instead of direct cash payments in shops and restaurants.

Credit Cards
All major credit cards are widely accepted. The tourism authorities suggest that if shops insist on adding a credit card surcharge (which they should not do), you

contact the relevant credit company in Singapore. Most hotels and car-hire companies will insist on a credit card and will probably demand full payment upfront if you cannot produce one. For 24hr card cancellations or assistance, call:

American Express	☎ 6538 4833
Diners Club	☎ 6294 4222
MasterCard	☎ 6533 2888
Visa	☎ 1 800 345 1345

ATMs
Most automatic teller machines will accept Visa, MasterCard and cards with Plus or Cirrus. ATMs can be found in most large shopping centres and MRT stations.

Changing Money
You can change money at banks and money changers. You'll find the major banks in the CBD and along Orchard Rd; their service fees for exchange are $2-3. Moneychangers offer better rates, don't charge fees and are located in almost every shopping centre in Singapore; ensure you use one that is licensed. Most shops accept foreign cash and travellers cheques at a slightly lower rate than you'd get from a moneychanger. Most banks are open Mon-Fri 9.30am-3pm, Sat 9.30am-12.30pm.

Tipping & Bargaining

Tipping is prohibited in the airport and discouraged in major hotels and restaurants where a 10% service charge is included in the bill. Elsewhere a 'thank you' tip for good service is up to you.

Many shops and department stores have fixed prices for clothes and luxury items. At markets, antique stores and electronics shops where prices are not displayed you can expect to bargain.

Discounts

In theory discounts for public transport and for tourist attraction entry are available for children under 12 or under 90cm tall, senior citizens over 60 and students. However discount rates do not always apply to non-Singaporeans. If you fall into any of the aforementioned categories it is best to present your student card or passport proving your age and ask if you are eligible. Ask the STB about current promotions during your stay.

Travel Insurance

A policy covering theft, loss, medical expenses and compensation for cancellation or delays in your travel arrangements is highly recommended. If items are lost or stolen, make sure you get a police report straight away – otherwise your insurer might not pay up.

Opening Hours

Opening hours for shops and offices vary. Generally, government offices are open from Mon-Fri 9am-5.30pm with a possible break for lunch, and Sat 10am-1pm. Major stores are open from around 10.30am-9pm, small shops operate from 10am-6pm. Many small shops, except those in Little India, are closed Sundays. Bank hours are approximately Mon-Fri 9.30am-3pm, Sat 9.30am-noon.

Public Holidays

Jan 1	New Year's Day
Jan/Feb	Chinese New Year (two days)
Mar/Apr	Hari Raya Haji
Mar/Apr	Good Friday
May 1	Labour Day
Apr/May	Vesak Day
Aug 9	National Day
Nov	Deepavali
Dec 25	Christmas Day

Time

Singapore is 8hrs ahead of GMT/UTC (London), 2hrs behind Australian Eastern Standard Time (Sydney and Melbourne), 13hrs ahead of American Eastern Standard Time (New York) and 16hrs ahead of American Pacific Standard Time (San Francisco and Los Angeles).

At noon in Singapore it's:

11pm in New York (the previous day)
8pm in Los Angeles (the previous day)
4am in London
6am in Johannesburg
5pm in Auckland
2pm in Sydney

Electricity

Electricity supplies are reliable and run at 220V to 240V and 50 cycles. Plugs are of the three-pronged, square-pin type used in the UK. Bring your own adaptors.

Weights & Measures

Singapore uses the metric system, though you may occasionally come across references to odd measurements, such as the *thola,* an Indian weight, or *batu,* the Malay word for mile (literally meaning 'stone'). See the conversion table, p. 122.

Post

Postal delivery in Singapore is very efficient and plentiful post offices also provide public phones, packaging materials and financial services. Call ☎ 1605 for the closest branch or try e www.singpost.com.sg.

Handy outlets include: Comcentre at 31 Exeter Rd (4, D8; open Mon-Sat 9am-9pm); #04-15 Takashimaya, Ngee Ann City, 391 Orchard Rd (4, C6; ☎ 6738 6899); and Terminals 1 & 2, Changi airport (2, E14; open 8am-9pm).

Postal Rates
Airmail postcards and aerograms cost 50c to anywhere in the world. Letters cost 70c-$1.

Opening Hours
Generally post office hours are Mon-Fri 8.30am-5pm, Sat 8.30am-1pm.

Telephone

Singaporean telephone numbers have eight digits. You can make local and international calls from public phones. International calls can be made from booths at the Comcentre (4, D8) 24hrs a day and at selected post offices. Most phone booths take phone cards, and some take credit cards, although there are still some coin booths around. For inquiries see ℮ www.singtel.com.

Phonecards
Local phone cards are widely available. Lonely Planet's eKno Communication Card, specifically aimed at travellers, provides competitive international calls (avoid using it for local calls), messaging services and free email. Log on to ℮ www.ekno .lonelyplanet.com for information on joining and accessing the service.

Mobile Phones
Mobile phone numbers in Singapore are generally prefixed 011 or 010. If you have 'global roaming' facilities with your home provider, your GSM digital phone will automatically tune into one of Singapore's two digital networks, MI-GSM or ST-GSM. There is complete coverage over the whole island and phones will also work in the underground sections of the MRT rail network. Rates vary and SMS messaging is cheaper than calling.

Country & City Codes
Republic of Singapore ☎ 65

Useful Numbers
Local Directory Inquiries	☎ 100
International Directory Inquiries	☎ 104
International Operator	☎ 1635
Weather	☎ 6542 7788

International Direct Dial Codes
Dial ☎ 001 followed by:

Australia	☎ 61
Canada	☎ 1
Indonesia border towns	☎ 011
Japan	☎ 81
Malaysia (STD)	☎ 020
New Zealand	☎ 64
South Africa	☎ 27
UK	☎ 44
USA	☎ 1

Electronic Resources

If you plan to travel with your notebook or palmtop computer, you will need a plug adaptor; Singapore uses the three-pronged, square-pin type used in the UK. Also, the telephone socket may be different from what you use at home; purchase a US RJ-11 telephone adaptor to convert to the local variety.

Internet Service Providers
Major Internet service providers such as AOL (℮ www.aol.com), CompuServe (℮ www.compuserve .com) and AT&T Business Internet Services (℮ www.attbusiness.net/) have dial-in nodes in Singapore.

Internet Cafes
Most 'Internet cafes' in Singapore are not cafes and they provide Internet services only. Many places offer computer games so outlets can be noisy. Access rates are around $3 per hour, in addition to those below you can also access the Internet at the National Library on Stamford Rd and Changi airport. If your hotel doesn't have Internet facilities it should be able to recommend

something close by, otherwise, try these:

Chills Cafe
#01-07 Stamford House, 39 Stamford Rd (3, H6; ☎ 6883 1016)

CoolSurfers.com
#01-02 Far East Square, 26 China St (3, L5; ☎ 6337 0075)

CyberStar Com Centre
#01-01 Beach Centre, 15 Beach Rd (3, G7; ☎ 6334 1232; open 24hrs)

i-surf
#02-14 Far East Plaza, 14 Scotts Rd (4, A5; ☎ 6734 3225; e isurf@isurf.com.sg; open 11am-11pm)

Red Spot Internet Cafe
#01-03 Singapore Finance House, 470 North Bridge Rd (3, G7; open 10am-11pm)

Useful Sites

The Lonely Planet website (e www.lonelyplanet.com) offers a speedy link to many of Singapore's websites. Others to try include:

Changi International Airport
e www.changiairport.com.sg

Happening Singapore
(arts, entertainment)
e www.happening.com.sg

Singapore Government
e www.gov.sg

Singapore Tourism Bureau
e www.newasia-singapore.com

The Straits Times
e www.straitstimes.asia1.com.sg

CitySync

CitySync Singapore, Lonely Planet's digital guide for Palm OS handheld devices, allows quick searches, sorting and bookmarking of hundreds of Singapore's attractions, clubs, hotels, restaurants and more – all pinpointed on scrollable street maps. Purchase or demo CitySync Singapore at e www.citysync.com.

Doing Business

Singapore is well equipped to assist business travellers and even Changi airport provides a useful business hub with free, wireless Internet access. Business travellers may find the following services of use.

For photocopying and printing try Fuji Xerox (#18-01 Suntec Tower 4, 6 Temasek Blvd; 3, G8; ☎ 6766 8888; e fxsgp1@signet.com.sg).

For answering, secretarial, administration and financial services try Classic International Pty Ltd (#06-322 The Plaza, 7500A Beach Rd; 3, F9; ☎ 6294 1100, fax 6296 6629; e sharlene@signet.com.sg).

The Executive Centre (#15-01, 30 Cecil St; 3, N5; ☎ 6232 2777; e www.executivecentre.com, sing@executivecentre.com) has fully equipped conference rooms as well as furnished offices for short- and long-term rental .

The best place to direct any business inquiries is the Singapore Trade Development Board (STDB; 07-00 Bugis Junction Tower, 200 Victoria St; 3, F7; ☎ 6337 6628). The STDB also has representatives at many of its overseas missions. Alternatively contact the Singapore International Chamber of Commerce (#01-01 John Hancock Tower, 6 Raffles Quay; 3, M6; ☎ 6224 1255, fax 6224 2785).

Newspapers & Magazines

The press is theoretically free but government crackdowns are possible and self-censorship is the norm. International English press publications, such as *Time* and *Newsweek* are readily available. Borders bookshop carries the best supply. For local news see *The Straits Times* or for fun try the tabloid *New Paper*. For entertainment see *8 Days*, *I-S* and *Juice* magazines. For live music try *Big O* magazine. Lifestyle magazines include *Her World* and the stylish *Men's Folio*. *Ex-pat* is suited to long-term visitors. Gourmets should see Tatler's *Singapore's Best Restaurants*, *Wine & Dine,* or *Makansutra* for hawker stalls. For comedy and local satire see **e** www.talkingcock.com.

Radio

English-language radio stations include BBC World Service (88.9FM), Class (95FM), Gold 90.5 (FM), News Radio (93.8FM), Perfect Ten (98.7FM), Symphony (92.4FM), the arts station Passion (99.5FM) and pop station Power (98FM).

TV

Most good hotels offer cable services in addition to local channels 5 (English), 8 (Mandarin) and 12 (Tamil and Malay), and the Arts Central channel. Check *The Straits Times* for programming details.

Photography & Video

You'll find a photographic processing outlet in most shopping malls. For professional services refer to the *Yellow Pages* for the most convenient outlet.

Singapore uses the PAL video format which is used in most of Europe and in Australia.

Health

Immunisations
Check with your doctor regarding immunisation requirements; you may consider immunisation against Hepatitis A. Visitors who have travelled from areas where yellow fever is endemic (Africa, South America) during the last six days will have to produce a vaccination certificate or submit to health screening.

Precautions
You may drink tap water everywhere in Singapore except Pulau Ubin. The weather in Singapore is hot and humid so ensure you are well hydrated and rested. Be alert to dehydration, sunburn, sunstroke, heat exhaustion, prickly heat and diet-related stomach upsets.

Insurance & Medical Treatment
Travel insurance is advisable to cover any medical treatment you may need while in Singapore. The standard of health care in Singapore is excellent; if you need medical attention ask your hotel for the nearest doctor or pharmacist. Major hotels will have a 24hr doctor on call. Otherwise, a trip to a community health centre for a tummy ache may only cost $20 while a trip to ex-pat orientated services will cost substantially more.

Medical Services
Hospitals with 24hr accident and emergency departments include:

Gleneagles Hospital
  6A Napier Rd (2, F8; ☎ 6473 7222)
Mount Elizabeth Hospital
  3 Mount Elizabeth Rd (4, B6; ☎ 6737 2666)
Raffles SurgiCentre,
  182 Clemencau Ave (3, G4; ☎ 6334 3337)
Singapore General Hospital (public)
  Outram Rd (3, N1; ☎ 6321 4113)

Dental Services
If you chip a tooth or require emergency treatment consult the *Yellow Pages*, ask your hotel for advice or call one of the hospitals listed above.

Pharmacies
There are pharmacies in every shopping mall and department store;

opening hours are approximately 9am-9pm and registered pharmacists usually work 9am-6pm. For emergencies contact the hospitals listed on p. 119).

Toilets

Most tourist attractions (excluding temples) and shopping centres have public toilets – some demand small change. All restaurants have toilets although the standards at hawker stalls may not be ideal. You'll also find toilets at popular recreation spots, like the East Coast Park. Otherwise, public toilets are difficult to find. You may have a choice between a sit-down and a squat toilet. A squat toilet may need to be flushed with a bucket of water. Older systems don't cope well with toilet paper – never put sanitary items down any toilet. Many toilets are self-flushing. You can be fined for not flushing.

Safety Concerns

Thanks to heavy penalties Singapore has a low level of crime and both sexes can feel fairly confident walking at night. However, pickpockets sometimes target tourists and gang fights have been known to break out at Boat Quay and in the alleys behind Orchard Rd at night. Use common sense and you're unlikely to encounter problems. Unless you're hankering for a jail sentence or even execution, do not import, take or sell drugs in Singapore or associate with anyone who does.

Lost Property

MRT	☎ 1800 336 8900
(or ask at information desks)	
Changi Airport	☎ 1800 541 2107/8
SBS Bus Services	☎ 6383 7211
Tanglin Police Station	☎ 6391 0000

Keeping Copies

Make photocopies of all your important documents, keep some of them with you, separate from the originals, and leave a copy at home. You can also store details of documents in Lonely Planet's free online Travel Vault, which is password-protected and accessible worldwide. See [e] www.ekno.lonelyplanet.com.

Emergency Numbers

Ambulance/ Fire	☎ 995
Police	☎ 999
Rape Crisis	☎ 1800 774 5935
& Women's Help Line (AWARE: Association of Women for Action and Research; Mon-Fri 4-10pm)	

Women Travellers

Singaporean women enjoy a high degree of autonomy and respect. Singapore is one of the safest destinations in South-East Asia and sexual harassment is less common than it probably is in your home country. Women may find the sheer number of men in Little India, especially on Sunday nights, to be a little overwhelming, but again there's really very little risk.

Tampons and contraceptive pills are readily available.

Gay & Lesbian Travellers

Homosexuality is illegal in Singapore and you can be sentenced to between 10 years and life for engaging in homosexual activities. Nonetheless the authorities generally turn a blind eye to the queer scene although gay clubs are sometimes targeted for 'overcrowding'. Singaporean entertainment venues are already cashing in on the 'pink dollar' and as the trend gains momentum it seems that persecution of lesbians and gays will become less likely.

Singaporeans are quite conservative about displays of public affection; women and straight Indian men can get away with same-sex hand holding, but an overtly gay couple doing the same would attract attention. It is unlikely however that you will encounter vocal or aggressive homophobia.

Information & Organisations

The Utopia website at **e** www .utopia-asia.com covers gay issues across Asia, although the site seems prone to breakdowns. The **e** www.fridae.com website provides excellent coverage of lesbian events and activities in Singapore and across Asia. Gay men should see **e** www.sgboy .com for local happenings and hangouts.

Senior Travellers

Asian cultures are very respectful of older people and Singapore is an ideal destination for senior travellers who want to experience a taste of Asia without the hassles of less-developed countries. The health care system is on a par with any Western country, access facilities to hotels and restaurants are excellent and there is a wide range of tours to cater for all tastes.

Singapore is a remarkably safe city and it's very easy to get around on public transport. The humid weather, however, can prove tiring – although travellers on guided tours tend to spend most of their time in air-conditioned buses or buildings.

The STB publishes a booklet called *Mature Travellers* with travel tips and occasional promotions.

Disabled Travellers

Most major hotels, tourist attractions and shopping malls, especially those along Orchard Rd, have good wheelchair access, however the crowded, narrow footpaths in Little India and Chinatown will prove challenging to anyone with mobility, sight or hearing issues. Venues may claim to have disabled access but once arrived you may find yourself expected to walk; if in doubt call first. Taxis are plentiful, the MRT is wheelchair friendly and Singaporeans are happy to help out.

Information & Organisations

Access Singapore is a useful guidebook for the disabled, produced by the Singapore Council of Social Services and available from STB offices (see Tourist Information p. 114) or contact the National Council of Social Services, ☎ 6336 1544, fax 336 7732.

Language

Singapore's official languages are Malay, Mandarin, Tamil and English; many Singaporeans speak several languages. Most people speak excellent English, although elderly and poorly educated people may not. Communication difficulties can arise due to the mutual incomprehensibility of one another's accents. To overcome this speak a little slower (not louder), smile and stay cool – getting excited will exacerbate the problem. Locals also speak the colloquial Singlish – a slang mix of English, Malay and Hokkien. See p. 12 for some of the more outrageous examples. Attempting to speak the local languages will endear you to locals, although they may also enjoy some laughs at your expense. You may like to invest in Lonely Planet's *Mandarin phrasebook*.

Conversion Table

Clothing Sizes
Measurements approximate only; try before you buy.

Women's Clothing

Aust/NZ	8	10	12	14	16	18
Europe	36	38	40	42	44	46
Japan	5	7	9	11	13	15
UK	8	10	12	14	16	18
USA	6	8	10	12	14	16

Women's Shoes

Aust/NZ	5	6	7	8	9	10
Europe	35	36	37	38	39	40
France only	35	36	38	39	40	42
Japan	22	23	24	25	26	27
UK	3½	4½	5½	6½	7½	8½
USA	5	6	7	8	9	10

Men's Clothing

Aust/NZ	92	96	100	104	108	112
Europe	46	48	50	52	54	56
Japan	S		M	M		L
UK	35	36	37	38	39	40
USA	35	36	37	38	39	40

Men's Shirts (Collar Sizes)

Aust/NZ	38	39	40	41	42	43
Europe	38	39	40	41	42	43
Japan	38	39	40	41	42	43
UK	15	15½	16	16½	17	17½
USA	15	15½	16	16½	17	17½

Men's Shoes

Aust/NZ	7	8	9	10	11	12
Europe	41	42	43	44½	46	47
Japan	26	27	27.5	28	29	30
UK	7	8	9	10	11	12
USA	7½	8½	9½	10½	11½	12½

Weights & Measures

Weight
1kg = 2.2lb
1lb = 0.45kg
1g = 0.04oz
1oz = 28g

Volume
1 litre = 0.26 US gallons
1 US gallon = 3.8 litres
1 litre = 0.22 imperial gallons
1 imperial gallon = 4.55 litres

Length & Distance
1 inch = 2.54cm
1cm = 0.39 inches
1m = 3.3ft = 1.1yds
1ft = 0.3m
1km = 0.62 miles
1 mile = 1.6km

lonely planet

Lonely Planet is the world's most successful independent travel information company with offices in Australia, the US, UK and France. With a reputation for comprehensive, reliable travel information, Lonely Planet is a print and electronic publishing leader, with over 650 titles and 22 series catering for travellers' individual needs.

At Lonely Planet we believe that travellers can make a positive contribution to the countries they visit – if they respect their host communities and spend their money wisely. Since 1986 a percentage of the income from books has been donated to aid and human rights projects.

www.lonelyplanet.com

For news, views and free subscriptions to print and email newsletters, and a full list of LP titles, click on Lonely Planet's award-winning website.

On the Town

A romantic escape to Paris or a mad shopping dash through New York City, the locals' secret bars or a city's top attractions – whether you have 24 hours to kill or months to explore, Lonely Planet's On the Town products will give you the low-down.

Condensed guides are ideal pocket guides for when time is tight. Their quick-view maps, full-colour layout and opinionated reviews help short-term visitors target the top sights and discover the very best eating, shopping and entertainment options a city has to offer.

For more indepth coverage, **City guides** offer insights into a city's character and cultural background as well as providing broad coverage of where to eat, stay and play. **CitySync**, a digital guide for your handheld unit, allows you to reference stacks of opinionated, well-researched travel information. Portable and durable **City Maps** are perfect for locating those back-street bars or hard-to-find local haunts.

'Ideal for a generation of fast movers.'

– Gourmet Traveller on Condensed guides

Condensed Guides

- Amsterdam
- Athens
- Bangkok
- Barcelona
- Beijing (Sept 2003)
- Berlin (Sept 2003)
- Boston
- Chicago
- Dublin
- Florence (May 2003)
- Frankfurt
- Hong Kong
- Las Vegas (May 2003)
- London
- Los Angeles
- Madrid (March 2003)
- New Orleans (March 2003)
- New York City
- Paris
- Prague
- Rome
- San Francisco
- Singapore
- Sydney
- Tokyo
- Venice
- Washington, DC

index

See also separate indexes for Places to Eat (p. 126), Places to Stay (p. 127), Shops (p. 127) and Sights with map references (p. 128).

PLACES TO EAT

PLACES TO STAY

SHOPS

sights – quick index